What Otl
Give
Parenting with Comp

"Kim Fredrickson's new parenting book is a compilation of some of the most effective parent training materials I have ever been exposed to. I have had the privilege of sitting in her classes and teaching alongside her. You will find the material and advice to be practical, based on sound research, and easy to understand. Parents regularly comment that Kim's teaching frees them to experience child care in a more positive and meaningful light."

—**Kenneth Logan**, PsyD, Psychologist and Professor of Counselor Education, Western Seminary, Portland

"Kim's wise advice helped me learn how to validate a teen's opinion even when I disagreed with him or her. I learned to move from teaching teens to coaching them. These skills and others helped me to foster true relationships with my own children and now enhance my relationships with them as adults. In fact, the concepts are so valuable, I use these same skills to inform my counseling practice."

—**Carol Karkazis**, Licensed Marriage and Family Therapist

"Kim shares practical advice that is simple, makes sense, and is something you can do. Her motto regarding parenting is 'It's all about the relationship,' and she offers guidance to develop a compassionate relationship with your kids. Her principles are in line with raising responsible and respectful children.

"Some of the best advice that I received from Kim was how to deal with a toddler in the store who wants something that you do not want to buy. When your child asks for something, don't just tell them no, which is what I would do. Kim suggested that I engage my daughter with questions as to why she wants that toy, what she likes best about it, how would she play with it and with whom. Brilliant! Instead of getting into a negative exchange, this was a positive interaction where I would actually learn more about my daughter and why she liked said toy. It deepened my relationship with my daughter, and I didn't buy the toy. I used this with ALL of my children!"

—**Betty K.**, Sacramento, CA

"The information I learned in Kim's parenting classes taught me that I needed empathy toward my teens. She shared a lot of practical advice that helped me so much. One that stands out is realizing that when I asked my teens, 'Why did you do that?' and they responded, 'I don't know,' that it was an accurate response, not a defiant response. I was able to use empathy rather than anger when I responded to them. I'm glad you wrote this book! The wisdom I received really made a difference in my parenting."

—**Dawn E.**, Sacramento, CA

"I have benefited greatly from your wisdom, Kim. I think of you often when I 'bite my lip' so that I can listen more and speak less!

"Your wisdom where my strong-willed child was concerned was life changing to him and to me. In your classes, you encouraged parents to respond with empathy in an emotionally charged talk with their kids. It never made sense to be empathetic and understanding of my child's challenging behavior. I would have to coach myself to keep implementing your words so I would get the best results. I couldn't believe I was able to be compassionate and empathetic when he simply would not comply! It always worked—but was so frustratingly counterintuitive.

"Thank you for teaching an emotion-charged mom how to be objective in the middle of crisis. I was able to show love and direct my kids in a (sometimes) gentle way. Thanks so much for writing this book. I am sharing it with the world."

—**Debbie B.**, Rocklin, CA

"The information shared in your parenting classes have helped me so much. Learning how to emotionally connect with my children has made such a difference in our family. My home is calmer, and I have better relationships with my four children. I especially appreciate you grounding your teaching in the Scriptures."

—**Laurie T.**, Sacramento, CA

"Thank you so much for your wise parenting advice. My children are in their early twenties. I recently started to use what you shared about listening and empathizing with my grown children, and they are opening up to me like never before. I'm so encouraged that it's never too late to strengthen my relationships with my children!"

—**Diane B.**, Sacramento, CA

"Thanks for helping us learn how to set clear boundaries with our 'spirited child.' We've been able to set compassionate boundaries with our son, and it is going well. He doesn't like it, but he is learning that we aren't 'pushovers' anymore."

—**Mary and Tom W.**, Roseville, CA

"I so appreciate your encouragement that even if our kids are older we shouldn't feel guilty for all the things we didn't do. That has helped me focus on moving forward and rebuilding the relationships with my children. I know it will take time, but I'm already seeing them warm to me a little. Thanks for giving me hope."

—**William J.**, Granite Bay, CA

"Kim Fredrickson understands intimately the liberating discipline of God, whose parent heart instructs us with great mercy and care, how to cultivate secure and empowering connections in the home. Kim offers great insights and practical guidance to grow your faith relationship with the LORD and wisely teach your children how to seek, know, and do the will of God in a cyber-powered world that inspires anxiety and doubt."

—**Joanna Jullien**, Founder and CEO, coreconnectivity.com

Give Your Kids a Break:

Parenting with Compassion for You and Your Children

Kim Fredrickson

Give Your Kids a Break: Parenting with Compassion for You and Your Children

Published by Kim Fredrickson. MFT

Printed in the United States of America

Library of Congress Control Number: 2017913414

Includes bibliographical references.

ISBN-13: 978-0-9888339-1-3

The author has spoken on these topics via her counseling practice over the last thirty years. She had made every effort to give credit where credit is due.

Most of the stories shared in this book are from Kim's life, with permission from her family. Other stories are a composite of the many situations parents and children find themselves in. No story is a direct reflection of a particular person.

This publication is intended to provide helpful and informative material on the subjects addressed. The author and publisher shall not be liable for your misuse of this material.

The author and publisher do not guarantee that anyone following these techniques, suggestions, tips, ideas, or strategies will become successful parents or have trouble-free children. The author and publisher expressly disclaim responsibility for any adverse effects arising from the use or application of the information contained in this book.

THIS BOOK IS dedicated to my children and future grandchildren. How I wish I could be here to help you as parents and be a grandma to your little ones. I write these words with deep love and care and a desire to be a part of your life in this way.

I love you and my future wonderful, amazing grandchildren. Give them extra love and hugs for me!

I trust these words will help all who read them. I urge you to parent in a way that puts your relationship with your children as the foundation for all else that comes. Parenting is beautiful, hard, delightful, exhausting, and a wonderful source of joy in your life.

"Trust in the LORD with all your heart and lean not on your own understanding; in all your ways submit to him, and he will make your paths straight" (Proverbs 3:5–6).

Seek God to help you with all the unknowns and challenges of parenting. He loves you deeply, and He loves your children even more. Turn to Him for strength, wisdom, and comfort. My love to you…always.

Contents

Acknowledgments

FIRST, I'D LIKE to thank God for sustaining me over a very difficult four years, battling two life-threatening illnesses. Throughout this unwanted journey, He has sustained and strengthened me, encouraged me, and provided many people who prayed and helped me in so many ways. He also provided me a way to still influence others through writing, and prompted me to write this book, which you can read more about in the foreword.

Special thanks to my husband, Dave, for his unwavering, loving support to me over our thirty-nine years of marriage. These last four years have been rough, and I'm grateful for the many ways he's had to adjust. I couldn't have made it without you.

Thanks so much to my agent, Wendy Lawton, with Books and Such Literary Agency, for all of your encouragement. Much appreciation to my editor, Jill Amack, for her excellent work to make this book even better.

Much appreciation to Rogena Mitchell-Jones, RMJ Manuscript Service, for such a superb job formatting the interior of my book and to Monica Haynes for the beautiful cover. Last, but not least, I am so grateful to Shayla Raquel for helping me launch my book to the world.

I appreciate your belief in me and support of this book. What a privilege it has been to partner with all of you.

Foreword

Why Write This Book?

I BEGAN THIS book as a way have an influence in the lives of my adult children and their future children. I wanted to help them with the challenges of parenting when the time came. Because of illness, I knew I wouldn't be around to hold my grandbabies and help my children raise them in person. I decided to write this book as a way of having a positive influence in their lives. Originally it was only going to be for them. As I wrote, I thought others might benefit as well, so I decided to publish it.

My health problems began four years ago, when I was diagnosed with breast cancer. I had the fast-growing kind that only 10 percent of people get. The treatment (lumpectomy, chemotherapy, and radiation) was grueling and much harder than I thought it would be. After nine months of treatment, I was all done and excited to get on with my life.

Four days after I finished treatment, I noticed I was having trouble taking a full breath. I went straight to the doctor, and after two months of tests I was diagnosed with pulmonary fibrosis, a lung disease, as a very rare side effect from the chemo and radiation—this only happens to 1–2 percent of people. Being special isn't all it's cracked up to be.

Pulmonary fibrosis is a terminal illness with a life expectancy of three to five years, and as of the publication of this book,

I've had it for three and a half years. It has been indescribably difficult and full of sorrow as I face a shorter life and what I'll miss with my husband, children, and future grandchildren. I had to close my counseling practice and get accustomed to using supplemental oxygen 24/7. As I worsen, I need more and more oxygen, and it gets harder and harder to leave home because I get so tired.

A blessing in all this is God's grace prompting me to still have a ministry to others from my recliner through writing and blogging. I have been a marriage and family therapist for thirty years, and for the last twenty years I've taught parenting workshops to thousands of parents. I decided to compile my favorite material into this book and add all I've learned about how important it is to have a compassionate relationship with ourselves. This is especially true as we parent our children. We desperately need compassion for ourselves. Our children also need to know how to be compassionate with themselves as they learn, fail, and grow.

Two years ago, I released my first book, *Give Yourself a Break: Turning Your Inner Critic into a Compassionate Friend.* In this book, I share how self-compassion helps us handle our humanness and the situations we are in with empathy, concern, understanding, and kindness. It also gives us the grace to accept and correct our mistakes.

Parenting with compassion is a gentle way we can relate to ourselves, especially when we're struggling with the demands of parenting. It makes such a difference to go through life with a kind friend on the inside rather than a critic who is telling us how we're messing up. Imagine what it would be like for you to have a compassionate friend inside to encourage you as a parent? Spoiler alert: It makes a huge positive difference!

I'm practicing self-compassion as I walk this journey from earthly life to eternal life.

I'm able to accept this new reality most of the time, cherishing everyday blessings and soaking in the good that is here now.

I look for ways to have an impact on my family, friends, and others as my time wanes. I'm intentional with my time and energy, and I try to be sensitive to God's leading. I'm giving my precious time and energy to this book, and I pray you will be blessed.

I also have the privilege of writing a blog about self-compassion and faith, as well as a weekly column to fellow pulmonary fibrosis patients that is read all over the world. I'm also working on a book to encourage those facing a terminal illness to be kind and compassionate with themselves on their final journey.

No matter what we go through, we can return to the hope that God is bigger than all the losses of life. No matter how long our inventory of losses may be, we can find in God a peace and hope that reshapes our struggle and gives us the strength to go on.

Many blessings to you as you learn to be compassionate with yourself as you parent the children God gave you. As you treat yourself with kindness, your children will learn to respond to themselves with compassion too. What a gift you are giving them for a lifetime!

—Kim

Kim's blog about self-compassion is at:
www.kimfredrickson.com/blog.
Kim's weekly column to pulmonary fibrosis patients and their families is at:
https://pulmonaryfibrosisnews.com/category/just-breathe-compassionate-help-for-the-pf-journey.

1

Self-Compassion for Parents

Praise be to the God and Father of our Lord Jesus Christ, the Father of compassion and the God of all comfort, who comforts us in all our troubles, so that we can comfort those in any trouble with the comfort we ourselves receive from God.

2 Corinthians 1:3–4

SHARON SANK TO the floor in the kitchen and burst into tears. She did it again, even though she promised she wouldn't. Her three-year-old son and five-year-old daughter found the egg carton in the refrigerator, and they dropped each egg on the floor with glee. They loved the sound each egg made as it cracked on the floor, and they giggled about how squishy they were.

Sharon wasn't amused. She'd only been in the bathroom a few minutes!

To add insult to injury, Sharon had just mopped the floor, and the egg carton was full. Sharon entered the kitchen after the last egg was dropped, and they were putting their little hands in the egg goo, ready to spread it elsewhere.

She yelled at them loudly, *"What are you doing? I just mopped the floor! What's wrong with you? You are a bad boy and bad girl. Go to your room!"*

Sharon watched their little faces, full of joy at their wonderful discovery, change into ones of sorrow and shame, and lots of tears. They ran to their room crying, and Sharon collapsed on the kitchen floor in tears.

Her anger turned on herself as she said, *"I yelled at them again; I promised I wouldn't. I can hear them crying. I'm such a bad mother. I didn't need to yell at them...but I just mopped the floor, and look at the mess I have to clean up. They're just kids. I'm such a loser, what's wrong with me?"*

Can you relate? I'll bet you could tell your own stories of losing it with your children and being harsh with yourself for being an imperfect parent. I know I can.

Here's the good news: we are all imperfect parents with imperfect children. We all deserve compassion, parents and children alike. As 2 Corinthians 1:3–4 states above, God has compassion on us and gives us comfort when we are struggling. He also gives us the ability to comfort our children as we walk through life together. He understands our struggles and has compassion for us. We can too.

Being a parent is one of the most wonderful things I have ever done in my life. It is also the hardest. Parenting requires more skills and knowledge than any job you will ever have. It is a job with little training and big consequences. Doctors spend seven to ten years of training in school and practice to make sure they are adequately prepared to hold the life of another person in their hands.

Parents are supposed to know it all, and we often hold multiple lives in our hands. We somehow need to possess emotional, social, physical, relational, and spiritual knowledge and skills to raise our children. There are no tests, training, or licenses to pass before bringing our first baby home from the hospital.

As parents, we all face special challenges being compassionate with ourselves and practicing self-care. We put on so many hats, support so many, and contribute so much to others in our lives. Yet, with all that effort, energy, love and investment in our work, families, church, and community we often feel disconnected, unappreciated, and worn out!

We Are Hard on Ourselves

WE CAN BE hard on ourselves. We don't mean to, we simply don't know another way to respond to our struggles and failures as a parent. We need compassion, not only for ourselves and the impossible job of being a parent, but for our children too. We have a lot in common with our children. We've never been a parent, and they've never been a child. We are all on a big learning curve.

Our culture can be quite hard on us as parents, passing judgment on how we help our children sleep, eat, go to school, and partake in extracurricular activities, to name a few. We live in a social media society where most things are edited, photoshopped, and presented as perfect. It's as if we think that there is a perfect formula to raise perfectly happy, perfectly achieving kids. Spoiler alert: there isn't!

As parents, we find it hard to be compassionate with ourselves for lots of reasons:

- Comparisons to other moms and dads…the list is unending
- Perfectionism
- Feeling that we are never enough

- Guilt and regrets
- Not taking time for self-care

We blame ourselves for being tired, for snapping at our kids, for not doing enough or for doing too much! We get down on ourselves for not knowing how to be a parent of a baby, a toddler, a grade schooler, or a teenager. The truth is that each stage of parenting has a huge learning curve, as does each child. Even if we parented other children, we haven't parented THIS CHILD before. Our high standards come from caring deeply for our little ones, but being hard on ourselves makes everything worse.

Take heart! We can learn to be compassionate with ourselves, as well as teach our children to treat themselves with kindness. This is called self-compassion, and I'll show you how.

So What Exactly Is Self-Compassion?

"Self-compassion is not self-pity, where we wallow in the shame of what we have done. It is not self-complacency, where we just accept where we are. Instead, it is the idea that we can be kind to ourselves when we fail and treat ourselves with the caring support we would give another who is struggling."[1]

Self-compassion factors in the truth that we make mistakes with the grace that understands I have worth and value, warts and all.

When we apply both grace and truth to ourselves, we take a look at what we did wrong without saying it's no big deal or saying it was a disaster. Applying self-compassion helps us handle our humanness and the situations we are in with empathy, concern, understanding, and kindness. It also gives us the grace to accept and correct our mistakes.

Self-compassion is a gentle way we relate to ourselves, both when we're struggling and when things are going well. We want to treat ourselves as we would a friend who is scared, confused, or learning something new.

Think about that last sentence. It's a description of how we feel as parents a lot of the time. Just when we figure out how to parent our two-year-old, he turns three. Right after we get the hang of parenting our twelve-year-old, she becomes a teenager! We are on a constant path of trial and error as we parent our children.

SELF-COMPASSION IS VITAL FOR A HEALTHY LIFE

LIFE CAN BE rough without the comfort, balance, and guidance of a self-compassionate friend on the inside. Lack of self-compassion affects our relationships and our well-being in profoundly negative ways. It makes such a difference to go through life with a kind friend on the inside rather than an internal critic or bully. Imagine what it would be like for you to have a compassionate friend inside to encourage you as a parent? I can tell you from experience that it makes a huge difference.

I became a parent never having babysat or changed a diaper. I knew some things about child development from my training as a counselor, but I had no actual experience with babies. When my mother-in-law came to help, she showed me how to do all the basics of caring for a baby. It was easy for me to emotionally attach to my firstborn son, for which I am grateful.

The problem was I didn't know how to interact with him. I asked her, *"What do I do with him when he's all fed, happy, and awake?"*

She told me to talk to him, read to him, and play little games with him. I had no idea, I'd never done it before.

I felt ashamed because I thought I should have known this. She didn't give me this message, I gave it to myself. Over several years, it became clear to me that there was no reason I should have known how to interact with a newborn. Where would I have learned this? Why should I have known? We can't know something we've never been taught or experienced. I learned as I went, and you can too.

Please keep this in mind as you read this book. I'd like to come alongside you as an experienced and imperfect mom and counselor, to help you parent with compassion, for yourself and your children.

I also want to share my experiences of failing, of not knowing, and of learning to have compassion for myself along the way.

We Need Self-Compassion to Parent Well

TREATING OURSELVES WITH compassion and kindness is extremely important as we go through the joys and stresses of parenthood. This applies even when you are crabby, yelled at your kids, have six piles of laundry, and forgot to send the diaper bag to preschool!

Self-compassion is a crucial practice for parents. If we continually give to others without nurturing ourselves, our emotional gas tank will be stuck on empty.

By nurturing and supporting ourselves, we will have more emotional resources to give to our children. By forgiving ourselves for the inevitable mistakes we make as parents—remembering we're only human and doing the best we can—we won't waste precious energy beating ourselves up.

Instead, we can learn from our mistakes and focus on the joy and meaning found in raising our little (or big) ones.

As our children see us model a nonjudgmental attitude toward ourselves when we make mistakes, it helps them handle their mistakes more easily. The honest truth is that we cannot teach our children what we do not know. This is why learning to be compassionate with ourselves is absolutely essential. We can tell our children to be compassionate with themselves all we want, but it won't have much effect if we can't accept our own imperfections.

When we don't know how to be compassionate with ourselves, we may default to blaming, shaming, and bashing ourselves. It is common to believe that being hard on ourselves helps us toe the line. The reality is that it doesn't, in fact it makes it worse!

Lack of self-compassion is linked to depression, anxiety, low self-esteem, problems in relationships, vulnerability to the opinions of others, and difficulty recovering from painful experiences.[2] Walking around with an inner critic who judges you for mistakes in the past and struggles in the present is quite depressing, and it produces a lot of anxiety. Imagine instead, that you have a compassionate friend on the inside who empathizes with you, helps you take care of yourself, and shows you how to be kind to yourself. Maybe this is hard to imagine right now, but it doesn't have to be.

The reality is that being a parent in this day and age is very challenging, no matter what the age of your children—young, teens, or adults. Your children at every age are experiencing different life challenges than we did. Not only is this hard and confusing for them, it requires a volume of skills, knowledge, and resources that no parent possesses, including myself. These ever-changing demands can result in us being unrealistically hard on ourselves about our ability to parent well in every situation.

The inability to be kind to ourselves also makes it harder to forgive ourselves and let go of mistakes. We may lose hope and begin to shut down emotionally. I don't know about you, but I've made lots and lots of mistakes as a parent. How could I not? It's unavoidable. We need a way to turn our inner critic into a compassionate friend.

Self-compassion helps to soothe our mistakes and regrets. It brings truth and grace to our hearts, helps us correct our mistakes, and repairs hurts with our children. It also gives us the freedom to learn what we don't know and find solutions.

Parents who practice self-compassion might say something like the following to themselves when they make mistakes, goof up, or regret their actions:

"Being an adult has many wonderful parts but also some really hard parts. Sometimes I feel like I don't know how to be a parent. Sometimes I'm confused about how to balance all my responsibilities at home, at work, and with friends. I have trouble knowing what to do or say about big topics like terrorism, the economy, the changing morals in our country, drugs, and a whole lot more. I have trouble being encouraging and following through on discipline.

"I'm starting to realize that most adults feel this way. It helps to know I'm normal. I think I'll be kind to myself about what I'm going through, rather than beat myself up about where I am struggling.

"I know I can find help from other parents and not have to figure all this out on my own. It feels good to know that, even if I'm not sure how, I can learn to be my own compassionate best friend."

Parenting is an indescribable blessing, and it also takes a lot out of us. We make lots of mistakes, and we also do lots of things right. You heard me! You are doing so much right already. We can all learn new ways to parent and fine-tune what is going well. Be kind to yourself along the way.

GIVE YOURSELF PERMISSION TO…

- Not know what you are doing
- Learn how to navigate this new life change, new baby, or new challenge
- Have mixed feelings about being a parent at times
- Be resentful, angry, hurt, and sad about not getting enough sleep or time to yourself
- Take time to gather information, talk to others, and seek help as you navigate through what is new and unexpected
- Learn how to be compassionate with yourself as you teach your children

SAY SOME KIND WORDS TO YOURSELF…

- I'm overwhelmed right now, and with good reason.
- I've never been through this before.
- I'll figure out how to do this new task a piece at a time.
- I'm not supposed to know how to handle something I've never been through before…no one does.
- I'll look for whatever little bits of encouragement and support I can see.
- I'll ask God and others for help, and look for unexpected answers.

ASK YOURSELF…

- Why do I think I should know how to help my children with a situation I've never handled before?
- Would I be down on my friend if I saw her do the same thing?
- What types of kind and compassionate words do I long to hear?

- What do I need my inner critic to stop saying?
- What is one supportive thing I could say to myself this week?

SELF-COMPASSION IS BIBLICAL

AS I SHARED in *Give Yourself a Break: Turning Your Inner Critic into Compassionate Friend*:

"Most people would agree that we are to be kind, considerate, helpful, and compassionate to others. But somehow this line of thinking breaks down when we decide how we are supposed to treat ourselves. Most of us would never treat others the way we treat ourselves: in the ways we talk to ourselves, care for ourselves, or help ourselves out when we are in need.

Fortunately, the Bible gives us solid teaching in Mark 12:28–31 when it tells us to love our neighbors as ourselves:

> *One of the teachers of the law came and heard them debating. Noticing that Jesus had given them a good answer, he asked him, "Of all the commandments, which is the most important?"*
>
> *"The most important one," answered Jesus, "is this: 'Hear, O Israel: The Lord our God, the Lord is one. Love the Lord your God with all your heart and with all your soul and with all your mind and with all your strength.'*
>
> *"The second is this: 'Love your neighbor as yourself.' There is no commandment greater than these."*

Ephesians 4:25–32 tells us how we are to love our neighbor, and therefore how to love ourselves:

Therefore, each of you must put off falsehood and speak truthfully to your neighbor, for we are all members of one body. "In your anger do not sin": Do not let the sun go down while you are still angry, and do not give the devil a foothold. Anyone who has been stealing must steal no longer, but must work, doing something useful with their own hands, that they may have something to share with those in need.

Do not let any unwholesome talk come out of your mouths, but only what is helpful for building others up according to their needs, that it may benefit those who listen. And do not grieve the Holy Spirit of God, with whom you were sealed for the day of redemption. Get rid of all bitterness, rage and anger, brawling and slander, along with every form of malice. Be kind and compassionate to one another, forgiving each other, just as in Christ God forgave you.

Based on these two Scriptures, we are to love ourselves in the following ways:

How we speak to ourselves:

- In truth, not lies.
- Without pent-up anger that causes us to sin.
- Building up, not tearing down.
- According to what is needed in the moment.
- With grace, not with clamor (yelling) and slander.

Ephesians 4:15 says,

"Instead, *speaking the truth in love*, we will grow to become in every respect the mature body of him who is the head, that is, Christ" (*emphasis added*).

- How we view ourselves: without bitterness, wrath, anger, and malice.
- How we provide for ourselves: working hard so we have something to share with ourselves and others.
- How we treat ourselves, especially when we make mistakes or sin: with kindness, tenderheartedness, and forgiveness.

Extending kindness to ourselves means we see ourselves as human beings who are wonderfully made by God and valuable, yet who are imperfect and make mistakes. This plays out in the way we view ourselves, speak to ourselves, listen to ourselves, care for ourselves, and respond to ourselves when we make mistakes. It also means learning to comfort ourselves and tending to our needs when we are hurt, lonely, tired, disappointed, sad, or angry. This may sound foreign to you because it is such a different way to approach yourself."[3]

Lack of Self-Compassion Hurts Our Relationship with God

AS A COUNSELOR for thirty years, I often heard clients say, *"I know God loves me and forgives me, but I can't feel it on the inside."* The problem is not with God. A part of us doesn't completely believe the goodness of God's love and forgiveness because we have a civil war going on inside ourselves. Often the critical part of ourselves rejects the truth of God's love, mercy, and forgiveness. Our inner critic won't let God's mercy, compassion, and forgiveness register deep within.

- Please know that it is not a conscious choice when we struggle in this way. Most likely we have never been shown how to relate to our weakness, sin, mistakes, and humanness in compassionate ways. When we struggle to take in God's love and mercy for us, we often beat ourselves up for not believing or trusting Him. The truth is, our struggle to accept the goodness of God has more to do with not being able to be compassionate with ourselves.

- When we can accept that there is both "good and bad" in ourselves, we can more readily develop true humility.
- When our internal critic is strong, we may hear our inner critic's messages above the Holy Spirit's. This happens when words of understanding, forgiveness, compassion, and direction from the Holy Spirit are blocked. This also occurs when our negative, unending internal comments mute the Holy Spirit speaking to us regarding sin in our lives.
- As we learn to be compassionate with ourselves, we will find a deeper, more loving, and more accepting relationship with God. What a gift this will be to yourself as well as your children!

I Have No Idea How to be Compassionate with Myself!

WHEN WE HAVEN'T learned how to be kind to ourselves, it is very common to think:

- I could never treat myself in such a positive way. What would I say?
- I have no idea how to start.
- I think being kind to myself applies to other people but not me.

I could do this in some areas but not an area I'm ashamed of.

Even if it doesn't feel like it right now, your worth and value is intact, despite mistakes you've made or regrets you have. I'd like to share some truths with you that you can read and take in…even a little bit at a time. Let's start by learning how to talk to yourself with compassion.

- Even though I make mistakes, do stuff wrong, and sometimes don't do the right thing, I am precious and valuable.
- Even though I wish I could go back and do some things differently with my children, I am still of great worth and value.
- Even with my faults and shortcomings, I am a person of worth, created by God.
- My problems, foibles, and failures do not shake up God. He has always seen me as valuable, and He always will.
- I can learn how to see and accept myself the way that God does. I can learn to treat myself with kindness, compassion, and grace.
- I can learn to heal the divide inside me and take in the value and love that God and others are extending toward me.
- Even when I mess up with my kids over and over, I can forgive myself and get help to handle these situations better in the future.

Notice how that feels. Don't worry if only some compassion goes in. That's normal. Just keep at it. You can learn how to end the civil war going on inside you and take in God's worth and value. You don't have to be stuck in this place. He truly does love you.

He truly does value you. And guess what, you can love and value yourself…a bit at a time.

Tools to Be More Compassionate with Yourself

Watch How You Speak to Yourself

SET BOUNDARIES WITH how you speak to yourself. No more putting yourself down, calling yourself names, or blaming yourself for what you did, didn't do, or should have done.

"I'm not going to speak to myself like this anymore. I don't quite know how to be compassionate with myself yet, but for now I'm going to stop talking to myself this way."

Instead of beating yourself up—approach yourself with compassion, saying, *"Wow—I really messed up, and I'm not happy about it. There are reasons I did this that I want to understand. I will take a look at why I snapped at my kids, and will change some things so I'm not so exhausted and on edge all the time. I can apologize and learn how to slow myself down next time. I'm an imperfect human being who is precious to God, and it's okay if I'm in process. This is not the end of the story."*

Approach Yourself in a Balanced Way

REMEMBER, THINGS ARE not as simple or explainable as they seem! Part of being compassionate with our shortcomings includes seeing just how complicated parenting can be. There are many factors in ourselves, our children, and our circumstances that all factor in to how we parent in specific situations. Very few situations are black and white.

"Yes, it is true that I yelled at my kids, haven't done the laundry, and drove through to get fast food again. It's also true that the kids are sick, I'm sick and haven't slept well, and I am feeling a lot of stress trying to make ends meet."

This balanced way of relating to ourselves means we acknowledge our less-than-perfect parenting, while at the same time also acknowledging the many circumstances that factored in to what we did or didn't do. We aren't excusing our mistakes. We are simply including compassion to the way we interact with ourselves.

"On the one hand, I've been short tempered and behind on everything! On the other hand, my husband is stressed [or I have no husband], my preschooler is having trouble adjusting to preschool, and I have a new baby.

"It's amazing I'm doing as well as I am. I'm going to see if there is anything I can do to get more support, let some things go, take some time for myself, and be an encourager to myself rather than beat myself up for what I'm doing wrong."

What would it be like if you responded to yourself in these compassionate ways? Seriously. My guess is you would feel calmer and accepting of yourself. You would be more resilient through the ups and downs of life. You'd enjoy your children more, and develop a friendship with yourself. Parenting is so much easier when you have a compassionate friend on the inside.

So how about it? We're in this together. We are all a mess. We love our kids, and we are doing the best we can.

There are definite ways we can improve how we parent, take care of ourselves, and live life.

This will be true until the day we die. How about being compassionate with ourselves as we parent the precious rascals God's given us?

Now What? Where Do I Start?

IT'S NOT TOO late to learn how to be compassionate with yourself. You can learn and grow alongside your children. Realize it is a process, and you are already on your way.

Here are a few tips to get you started:

1. Notice the way you talk to yourself. You can't change what you aren't aware of. You may be surprised how much time you spend saying negative things to yourself.
2. Say no to your inner critic! When your inner critic starts talking to yourself harshly, pause and say, *"I'm not going to talk to myself like that anymore."* This is a great step, even if you don't know a compassionate thing to say in its place. Over time you'll learn to say, *"I'm going through a really hard time right now. I am not going to criticize myself, even though that may be my first response. I can get help, apologize, and learn from my mistakes. No one, including God, expects me to be a perfect parent. There is a lot I'm doing right."*
3. Say the following to yourself: *"What would a kind friend say to me right now about how I goofed up?"*
4. Get help to learn how to be compassionate with yourself. Read about self-compassion and learn how to treat yourself differently a bit at a time. My book, *Give Yourself a Break: Turning Your Inner Critic into a Compassionate Friend*, is filled with stories about different scenarios we can all relate to. I share lots of examples of what it sounds like to use grace-filled compassionate language with yourself...kind of like having a self-compassion coach alongside you.

5. Take care of yourself. Make time to do things that are calming and soothing for you: relaxation, reading, walking in nature, doing your favorite hobby, time with affirming friends, whatever you have noticed brings you encouragement and comfort. Take steps to eat healthy and exercise in ways that work for you.

2

Teaching Your Children Self-Compassion

When he saw the crowds, he had compassion on them, because they were harassed and helpless, like sheep without a shepherd.

Matthew 9:36

I LOVE THIS verse. Notice what it says and doesn't say. It shows that Jesus saw that they were harassed and helpless, with no one to help. He responded with compassion and sought to meet their need. This verse doesn't say that Jesus was mad at them or blamed them for the mess they were in. No, He responded with compassion and help. What a wonderful model for us.

Parenting with Compassion

WHAT IS COMPASSION? It involves both sympathy and concern for the sufferings or misfortunes of others, as well as a desire to help. As we parent with compassion, we tune in to the unique needs and struggles of our children. We try to see the world through their eyes, factoring in their age, personality, and unique life challenges.

Our children desperately need to learn how to be compassionate with themselves. They are vulnerable to being hard on themselves because they are constantly learning new things, which involves lots of failure. When kids practice self-compassion, they become more resilient, feel better about themselves, and have a greater ability to handle life's problems.

Our children are growing up in a divided world. Our society is not governed by the morals, manners, and decency we grew up with. Society tells us that "anything goes and all is acceptable," and we need to adjust and accept all views, regardless of our personal beliefs and values.

These negative messages and pressure come at our children from all sides—from school, friends, and social media. It is normal for them to want to be accepted and included by their friends and social groups. They need a way to be their own kind friend and advocate as they are subjected to pressure, hurtful words, and opinions they don't agree with.

The reality is that our children will encounter people who disagree with them and don't like things about them for the rest of their lives. We need to equip them to handle and recover from the difficulties of life.

Practicing self-compassion helps our children do just this. Without it they are vulnerable to peer pressure and the opinions of others, and they might find it difficult to retain their own thoughts and feelings, and stand firm in their faith and convictions.

Self-compassion helps them step back and be kind to themselves after going through a difficult situation. They are then able to evaluate what they've been through and decide what they want to do about a given situation.

The Enemy of Self-Compassion = Shame

SOME RECENT RESEARCH[4] shows the long-term effects on children when they use shame self-talk versus guilt self-talk. They specifically wanted to know how children talked to themselves after doing something wrong. Researchers looked at a 380 fifth graders, and they measured whether these kids were using more shame self-talk or guilt self-talk. When doing something wrong, shame self-talk focused on "*I* did something bad," while guilt self-talk focused on "I did *something* bad." Big difference.

Those who shamed themselves for wrongdoing felt small, worthless, powerless, and exposed. Because shame hurts so much, they would do anything to not feel it, by denying responsibility or shifting the blame to someone else. They often became irrationally angry with others, aggressive, and destructive.

Those who felt guilty after doing something wrong experienced internal tension, remorse, and regret over the "bad thing done." These powerful feelings motivated these children to confess or apologize and learn from their mistakes.

The children who used shame self-talk felt like their sense of worth, value, and the ability to be loved was at risk when making a mistake. The children who used guilt self-talk felt like their bad behavior was the focus of needed change, not their very self.

This group of researchers interviewed these children again ten years later, when they were seniors in high school. What they found is incredibly important for us to understand. The shame-prone kids were more likely to attempt suicide, drop out of high school, struggle with eating disorders and depression, and engage in high-risk drug, alcohol, and sexual behaviors.

The guilt-prone kids, on the other hand, were more likely to finish high school, apply for college, engage in community activities, and engage in lower-risk drug, alcohol, and sexual behaviors.

Shame self-talk knows nothing of self-compassion. Remember, self-compassion is a balance of grace and truth. *"I love who you are, but the choice you made is not acceptable."* It's very important for our children's moral choices, future happiness, and success in life that we discipline without shame and teach self-compassion when we and our children fail. We'll be covering how to do this in chapters 5 and 6.

Fifteen-year-old Cammie felt like leaving school early…again. All the girls at lunch were comparing everything—from clothes to boyfriends to what they were doing this weekend. Cammie always felt like she came up short. Today, however, rather than hide in the bathroom for the rest of lunch and put herself down, Cammie decided to be nice to herself.

Her youth pastor shared on Sunday about treating yourself with grace and truth and coming to your own defense when things got tough. Cammie used to think that in order for her to feel good about herself she needed to be like the other girls and get their approval. This time she decided to take a walk and speak to herself kindly.

"It's really hard to hang out with a group that seems so perfect. It's really hard to feel like I don't measure up. I'm not going to be mean to myself this time. I'll take a big breath and comfort myself with the truth. I don't have the latest clothes or the cutest boyfriend...or any boyfriend. Those things don't make me worthless or less than. They make me a teenage girl who is trying to figure out how to do my life.

"I have many good qualities that matter. I am kind, loving, and smart. I care about people and God. I have friends at my youth group, and Pastor Mike and a bunch of the other kids said they were glad to see me on Wednesday. I think the problem is more about the kids I'm eating lunch with. I think I'll eat lunch with other kids who don't compare everything. Whew...I feel better now. I'm so glad I could be a friend to myself!"

How wonderful that Cammie could separate feeling bad from being bad. Sometimes we get confused about this. She felt bad because of some immature friends she was hanging around with who were also trying to figure out how to belong and feel of worth and value.

Cammie comforted herself when she felt bad without making herself feel as if she were bad. By turning toward herself with compassion, she became a compassionate friend to herself. This shift can make all the difference in the world!

You may be realizing you've been using shame to try to change your children's behavior because you haven't known what else to do. Most likely this is how you were parented, and how your parents were parented. Take a deep breath and know that it's not too late. We continue to parent our children in one way or another until the day we die. We can learn to influence our children without using shame. It's never too late, even if your children are adults.

The Difference Between Self-Esteem and Self-Compassion

OVER THE YEARS, there has been a huge emphasis in our society on building kids' self-esteem. Psychologists now think we should be teaching children how to develop self-compassion instead.[5] Self-compassion is different from self-esteem. Self-esteem develops by comparing yourself to others and assessing that you are better than they are. This can lead to narcissism (feeling special or better than others) and increase the chance that your child will feel devastated when she doesn't get the "A" or win the trophy.

Self-compassion, on the other hand, is a gentle way we relate to ourselves when we're struggling—with kindness, caring, empathy, and understanding. Self-compassion focuses on being kind to oneself while learning from life experiences. Our inherent value comes from being a unique creation of God, not because of our accomplishments.

Some worry that being compassionate with yourself will make you or your children turn into lazy bums. The opposite is actually true! Those who treat themselves with kindness are often more level-headed, work harder, and have higher standards than those who are critical of themselves. This makes sense. When we aren't fighting with a critical part of ourselves, we can settle down on the inside and move forward in areas that are important to us.

You Don't Need to Be a Perfect Parent!

WE HAVE A false belief that in order to have a positive impact in our children's lives, we need to do everything perfectly, or pretty close! This is just not true. We can have an even bigger impact in our children's lives when we goof up and apologize. It is in these moments that we show them how to live life as an imperfect person.

They need to see us apologize when we hurt someone, make amends in our relationships, and be compassionate with ourselves when we fail. None of that can be taught by words, only experience.

As a therapist, I worked hard to stay in tune with my clients and not make mistakes in how I responded to them in their most tender moments. Of course, try as I did, I still made mistakes, resulting in hurt feelings. I always felt bad about this, but it didn't paralyze me. I knew that it was in these vulnerable moments I could be a source of healing.

What I discovered was that many of my clients had never had anyone admit they misunderstood them or hurt them. Of course, this happened; it was unavoidable.

They didn't hear their parents openly acknowledge, *"I got that wrong, I let you down, I hurt you by what I said or did...and I'm so sorry."* Instead, their parents either didn't notice, pretended it was no big deal, or blamed their children for their bad actions.

I share this to give you hope. How you handle the mistakes you make with your children is the gateway to a deeper and more meaningful relationship. This is how you equip your children to live in a judgmental world that doesn't offer grace and understanding for mistakes.

As we learn to embrace our imperfections, we will help our children to do this as well.

Skills to Help Children Learn Self-Compassion

CHILDREN DESPERATELY NEED ways to be compassionate with themselves. Because they are constantly learning and growing, they often feel frustrated and inadequate about their abilities, especially as compared to others. It's common for them to criticize themselves over their academic performance, popularity, looks, and athletic ability.

Learning ways to process their thoughts and feelings, while treating themselves with compassion, builds a solid foundation for the future. Not only will these skills get them through childhood and adolescence, they will help them establish healthy relationships with themselves and others for a lifetime.

When kids practice self-compassion, they become more resilient, feel better about themselves, and have a greater ability to handle life's problems.

Here's a highlight of how to teach your children to be compassionate with themselves. These will be more fully developed in the rest of this book.

Model This Way of Relating to Yourself

WHETHER WE MEAN to or not, children learn how to treat themselves when they fail by watching us. That is hard to swallow, I know. I only want them to learn the good things from me!

Are you hard on yourself when you make mistakes? Do you get down on yourself about your looks and weight? Do you beat yourself up when things don't go well at work? Do you use harsh words to describe yourself? Are you critical about your emotions?

Don't worry, there is hope! As we learn to be compassionate with ourselves, they will pick this up as well. Our model to them is more powerful than anything we say. You don't need to have self-compassion nailed down yourself before you can teach your kids. We can be on the same journey with them.

Teach Awareness

OUR WORLD IS a fast-moving, distracting place. At any moment, we are drawn to our phones, TV, texts, and other media. We are burdened by all we need to do and feel pulled in a million directions. Our children are too. In order to develop compassion for ourselves and our children, we need to be aware of what's happening on the inside. The following are ways to help your children become aware.

- Pause. There's always so much going on. Encourage them to take a few breaths to slow down inside.
- Teach your kids how to be present with themselves. This includes noticing their thoughts and feelings, what's happening in their bodies, as well as what they need.

- Help them practice gratitude, soaking in positive experiences when they occur. It's so easy to focus on the negative.
- When difficult events happen, use them as moments to practice self-compassion.
- Some more tips to help are in chapters 8 and 9.

Encourage Kindness

OUR WORLD IS often not a very kind place. We want to teach our children that success is achieved through treating others with respect, kindness, and compassion…not through force and intimidation. This is also true of how they treat themselves.

Responding to ourselves with kindness and understanding when we struggle or fail is a core component of self-compassion. How we talk to ourselves in these vulnerable moments has a bigger impact on us than how others respond to us. The way we speak to our children is the model for how they communicate with themselves. Here are some ways to teach them to be kind to themselves:

- Don't talk to them in a critical or harsh way. Comment on what they did wrong without yelling or name-calling. "Mary, I'm upset that you didn't take out the trash as you promised. Please do it now."
- Next time your children say something critical, gently point this out to them. Help them distinguish between their worth versus what they did. Do they immediately go to, "I'm stupid, I'm a loser, I'm unlovable," or do they see what they did as a bad choice or a mistake?
- Help them think of a balanced way of looking at themselves when they make mistakes. Let's say in the above example Mary says, "I'm so stupid." Stop her and say,

"Mary, you're not stupid, you just didn't take out the trash. You can take care of that right now. Everyone forgets to do chores sometimes."

- Teach them how to self-soothe during difficult times. This means learning ways to calm themselves down when they are upset. Ideas include: taking some slow, deep breaths while saying, "I'm going to be okay," giving themselves a hug, or listening to soft music.
- Tell stories about children who made mistakes and then forgave themselves, were upset and calmed themselves down, or hurt someone else and apologized. I used to make up stories with my children's names doing just that.

Simply telling our children to treat themselves with compassion doesn't work. Teaching them to be kind to themselves through the everyday activities of life gives them the practice they need so that it becomes their norm. More practical ways to teach your children self-compassion are sprinkled throughout each chapter.

Remind Them That Others Struggle Too

- Let your children know that they are not the only ones having a hard time. Everyone struggles, feels inadequate, or fails at things in life. These messages help normalize what your children are going through and reduces their embarrassment when they struggle or fail.

It will help your children hear you say:

- "It is normal to feel frustrated and disappointed when things don't turn out as you hoped."
- "All of us feel jealous of others sometimes."

- "It makes sense that you are angry and hurt by what your friend said."

- Share with your children when you struggle too. While we are aware of our imperfections, our children often are not. It will help them know that you don't have it all together, and that you make mistakes too. This perspective will help them see themselves and others in a more realistic way.

They will be relieved to hear:

- "I did the same thing when I was your age."
- "I'm embarrassed that I was rude to the grocery store clerk."
- "I'm so sorry I didn't follow through. I told you I'd pick up the supplies you needed, and I didn't. I'm so sorry."

Don't worry, more tips to help your children realize they are not the only ones who struggle appear throughout this book.

LABEL AND VALIDATE FEELINGS

OUR EMOTIONS CAN be confusing and overwhelming. We often have no idea what to do with them, and we may be tempted to push them away.

Our children need us to help them label and validate their emotions. This will help them regulate their emotions and learn from them. Our emotions aren't the problem. What causes problems is when we don't know how to express them in ways that are healthy and safe.

Accepting our feelings, rather than judging or pushing them away them helps us learn from them and find solutions. This positive stance helps us be kind and compassionate with ourselves. We teach our children these skills in several ways:

- Labeling our own emotions helps them learn to label theirs. Simply saying, "I'm so sad about not getting together with my friend today" teaches them so much. They learn that it is normal to be sad when things don't work out.
- Sharing difficult feelings helps them see it is okay to talk about them. Saying them out loud takes away some of their power. It also helps them learn how to handle them. "I'm so frustrated that I can't get this project finished. I need to take a break." This models kindness to yourself, and shows your children there are ways to recover when frustrated.
- Validate and empathize with what they are going through. They have no idea what they are feeling and need our help. Simple validation of their emotions helps them learn and accept them.
  - "You seem very angry. Something hard must have happened."
  - "It's not like you to be mean to your brother. I wonder if you are having a hard day."
  - "It's not okay to hit your sister."
  - "I want to understand what happened."
- Read books together about emotions. Ask, *"How do you think that little boy was feeling? Have you ever felt the same way?"* You can also ask these types of questions when watching a show or movie.

These creative ways of teaching your children about their emotions lets them know their emotions are good and acceptable. As you strive to understand your children's point of view, your children will too!

This is another building block to help your children become a compassionate friend to themselves. We'll be covering more in chapters 3, 4, 8, and 9.

Discipline the Behavior, Not Your Children's Character

ONE OF THE most important jobs we have as parents is to convey our love and acceptance of our children, no matter their accomplishments or failures. We want to accept them for who they are, not for who we want them to be. This doesn't mean we allow bad behavior and let things go. What it does mean is that we focus on disciplining the behavior, not making negative statements about them as a person.

Children can't see the difference unless we make it crystal clear.

Saying, *"That was hurtful when you wouldn't let your friend pick what you were going to play,"* comments on the behavior you are unhappy with. This is in stark contrast to, *"You are a selfish person and don't care about your friend."* This distinction is also important to make with accomplishments.

I tried to praise my children's character rather than their grades. *"You worked so hard and didn't give up. I'm so proud of you."* This small difference makes it less likely that your children will confuse their accomplishments with their self-worth.

We'll be learning more about disciplining with compassion in chapters 5 and 6.

Apologize and Forgive

APOLOGIZING AND ASKING forgiveness teaches self-compassion in powerful ways. When our children see us apologize and ask forgiveness from them and others, it teaches them to do this as well.

There are powerful messages in this process that are life giving to your children.

- You did something wrong and aren't afraid to acknowledge it.
- Their feelings were hurt, and you are sorry that that happened.
- You care deeply about them and your relationship.
- You can acknowledge you were wrong without beating yourself up.
- Mistakes can be repaired; relationships can heal.
- If you can do this, so can they.

As parents, we make lots of mistakes; it's unavoidable. We can teach our children that mistakes don't have to ruin a relationship or cause them to hate themselves. They can be repaired, forgiven, and restored.

Now What? Where Do I Start?

IT'S NOT TOO late to learn how to teach your children to be compassionate with themselves. Realize it is a process, and you are already on your way. Here are a few tips to get you started:

1. Sit down with them and say, *"I'm learning about something new that makes sense to me, and I want to talk*

about this as a family. I was reading a book about how important it is to be kind to ourselves, especially when we mess up. I realized I'm not very good at this, and I want to get better at it. When I goof up, I tell myself I'm stupid. What about you? What do you say to yourself when you make a mistake?"

2. Set some ground rules regarding how family members talk to one another and themselves. Ask your kids their opinion too. Here are a few to start with:
   - No name-calling.
   - No hitting "below the belt" by teasing one another about weaknesses.
   - No making fun of what people say.
   - We'll learn more in chapter 11 about healthy ways to hold a family meeting.
3. When your child messes up and can't come up with kind words to say to herself, it can be helpful to have her think about the kindest girlfriend she knows. Then ask her, *"What would Mary say to you right now about how you messed up?"* or *"What would you say to Mary if she made the mistake you did?"* You'll be surprised how easily your kids will come up with compassionate words to say when we ask these types of questions.

3

Building Emotional Closeness with Your Children

Little children, let us not love with word or with tongue, but in deed and in truth.

1 John 3:18 (NASB)

PARENTING IS *HARD*. We face huge challenges trying to effectively parent in this ever-changing, difficult world. It is hard to live in, never mind raise children in.

Being a parent zaps us of everything—energy, finances, time, and sometimes even confidence. It also gives us indescribable joy.

Building emotional closeness with your children is the foundation upon which everything else is built.

Without a close emotional relationship, children will have trouble adopting our moral values, accepting discipline, and developing a solid self-esteem. We love our children and are willing to do almost anything for them.

Sometimes we don't know how to communicate our love in ways that sink down deep into our kids' hearts and souls.

Having a warm feeling in our hearts for our children is not enough. Telling them we love them is not enough. Loving them through actions that are meaningful to them carries far more weight than just the words we use.

Kids need practical, hands-on interactions to feel loved and that they belong.

Positive emotional interactions between parent and child have a huge impact on children's well-being and long-term success.

A solid emotional connection with your children is more important than the kind of discipline you use.

WHAT IS EMOTIONAL CLOSENESS?

> *"A bond between two people is an emotional and personal investment they have in one another.*
>
> *"It is a relationship in which all of the parts of the soul—feelings, needs, thoughts, values, beliefs, joys, and sorrows—are shared with and valued by another...*
>
> *"When we are bonded, we 'matter' to someone. When we are connected to another person, we feel that we make a difference to him, that our presence is desired when we are around and missed when we are absent.*
>
> *"This sense of 'mattering' is in direct contrast to feeling overlooked, forgotten, or even simply tolerated by others."*[6]

Think how powerful it would be to have this type of emotional connection with your children.

Imagine what would it feel like as a child to have this loving bond with your parents. This way of relating establishes a safe and secure foundation to handle the ups and downs of life.

WHAT DIFFERENCE DOES EMOTIONAL CLOSENESS MAKE?

IT MAKES A huge difference to the success and well-being of your child, as well as makes parenting easier. Studies[7] have shown that when children feel emotionally close to their parents, they:

- feel more content on the inside;
- have higher self-esteem;
- get sick physically less often;
- do better academically;
- get along better with friends;
- have fewer behavior problems;
- are less prone to acts of violence; and
- are less vulnerable to find a place to belong with peers.

When children feel connected emotionally on the inside, there are fewer power struggles and more joy.

It isn't enough to feel love for our children, we need to express it in ways our children can feel it, and meet their deep emotional needs.

It is important to ask ourselves, *"What types of words and activities cause my child to feel loved,"* not *"What makes me feel loved?"*

What Breaks Down Emotional Closeness?

Criticism of Who the Child Is, Not Just About What She Does

FOR EXAMPLE, YOUR child doesn't do her chores, despite your clear instructions. Unhelpful: "You are a lazy person and only care about yourself." Helpful: "You didn't do your chores. You will need to do them before you can play with your friends."

Not Spending Enough Connecting Time

TO KIDS, "LOVE" is spelled T-I-M-E. In our world, finding time is quite a challenge. They notice that what is important gets our time.

Out-of-Control Anger and Yelling

THIS APPLIES TO being yelled at, as well as seeing it happen to others. Experiencing out-of-control anger and yelling affects a child's sense of safety. It's hard to trust and feel close to others if you are afraid.

Excessive Discipline

THIS MEANS PUNISHMENT, not logical consequences for wrongs done.

Too Many Activities

NOT ENOUGH TIME for holding, talking, and discussion of their thoughts and feelings. What are their hurts and joys? What are their hopes and dreams?

What Builds Emotional Closeness?

Eye Contact

THE FIRST WAY that builds emotional closeness is eye contact. This is especially true for babies and young children. They suck in nurturing love this way, and they can maintain eye contact much longer than we can. This is because they don't get uncomfortable with intimacy the way we do.

It is important to give eye contact consistently. We want to give them eye contact whether we are pleased with them or angry with them. If we only make eye contact when our child "performs," we will inadvertently communicate conditional love. As a result, our child will feel he is a disappointment and our love hangs in the balance.

Teaching our children to be comfortable with eye contact will help them throughout their lives. Children who make eye contact make friends easier. When they are unable to, they may have difficulty relating to and connecting with others.

Physical Touch

THIS SEEMS SUCH an obvious way to convey love, but without knowing it, often the major amount of physical contact occurs out of necessity, such as changing diapers, getting dressed, or getting in and out of the car. Physical touch really fills a child's emotional tank. Hugs, kisses, holding hands, a touch on the shoulder, and a pat on the head all convey love in tangible ways a child can feel and soak in.

As children get older, they may want love expressed in different ways. Other ways might include a back scratch, a pat on the back or shoulder, wrestling, or sitting close while watching TV. These ways of expressing love communicate the message, *"You're loved. You're accepted. You matter."* This is not only important to your child in the moment, but it is foundation for them feeling loved in their adult relationships. If not, they may feel an emptiness inside, overly need affection, or be susceptible to substances, addictions, or unhealthy habits to fill the void. This can also set kids up to later become promiscuous or be drawn to false types of connection such as pornography.

From the time our kids were five to ten, we did a family snuggle every morning before school. We told them they could hop into our bed with us from 7:00 to 7:20 a.m. We hugged and talked, and it was a great way to start the day.

Focused Attention

THIS IS GIVING our children full, undivided attention in such a way that they feel without a doubt that they are completely loved. One-on-one time is vital to a good self-esteem and the ability to relate to and love others. Our homes are their school for relationship training, as well as others. Just like taking math or science in school, they learn to relate and do relationships at home.

Children do not do their best, feel their best, behave their best unless they are given focused attention. This is hard to do, especially when you have more than one small child at home. This means focusing on them and not multitasking, looking at our phone, TV, computer, or reading the paper at the same time.

Doing this takes planning and time and is often challenging to do. It is worth the effort though because without it, a child feels anxiety because he feels everything is more important than him.

Dr. Stanley Greenspan shares, in *Playground Politics,* an effective tool to create emotional closeness with younger children.

> *Floor time is a special unstructured time that you set aside for yourself and your child. During this time,*

> *about 30 minutes a day at a minimum, you get down on the floor with your child, trying to "march to your child's drummer." Obviously, with an older child, you might not literally be on the floor. You may be sprawled on a couch or sitting side-by-side on the back step, taking a walk, or sweating it out on the basketball court. But the goal, no matter where you are or what you are doing, is to follow your child's lead and tune in to whatever interests your child. In other words, for those daily 30 minutes, your child is the director—you are merely the assistant director. You follow her lead in play or conversation, only trying to support and amplify the direction your child is moving in.*
>
> *The idea behind floor time is to build up a warm, trusting relationship in which shared attention, interaction, and communication is occurring on your child's terms. Floor time is the most effective way I have found to accomplish this goal. When that warm, trusting relationship has begun to blossom, you are laying the groundwork for tackling any and all challenges that your child faces.*[8]

They decide what to play, even if it drives you crazy. What matters the most is spending time playing with them consistently, even if it is fifteen minutes a day.

If you have a lot of kids in your home, or your time is limited, pick a day for each child when you will spend one-on-one time with them. Focus on your child and what they are thinking and feeling.

Examples in our family of focused time: playing house, coloring, Nintendo, toys, LEGOs, Pokémon, Barbies, art, cooking, drawing, talking, playing sports with them, Ninja Turtles, and watching them play their favorite video game and talk about it.

They get the love and attention they need. This focused time tells them they are important.

They have at least a little time during the day to be in charge. It's the one time they aren't being told what to do, what to eat, or what to wear. It gives them time to show their initiative and have their own ideas.

VALIDATION WITH EMPATHY

THIS TYPE OF interaction seeks to connect with the thoughts and feelings of your child. It means putting yourself in their shoes…asking yourself the question, *"What must it be like to be my child in this situation?"* This is different than looking at the situation and asking yourself, *"What would I feel like in this situation?"* Your child will feel connected to you as you focus on understanding his thoughts and feelings. Validation with empathy involves reflecting back to your child the facts and feelings of what they've shared without trying to fix the problem. This helps meet the universal need that all of us have:

> *To believe I am of worth, my feelings matter, and someone really cares about me…all of us want to be listened to and understood. We want to be appreciated for who we are individually. We need to be heard completely and not judged, corrected, or advised. When those who are meaningful to us will not take the time to hear us out by genuinely listening, we experience a profound negative effect.*[9]

You want your children to know that their feelings matter and that you understand what they are going through. You want your comments to be kind, gentle, and respectful with the intent to truly care about and understand them. You want them to know, *"What you're feeling is okay, and I understand."*

Here are some ways to communicate this:

- "I know you are having a hard time..."
- "Is this a tough day for you?"
- "I know a part of you wants to do the right thing."
- "I care about how you are doing on the inside."
- "It's not like you to ____, I'm wondering if there is something else going on inside of you?"

We sometimes feel so bad for what they are going through that we want to jump in and make it better, or comment on the bright side.

We may feel like it's being helpful, but it isn't. What they need is for us to join them in their pain and not minimize what they are going through.

Helpful: "It's so hard to go to the dance and not be asked to dance."
Painful: "At least you got to go to the dance. My dad would never let me go."
Helpful: "You must have wanted to disappear when she made fun of you in front of all your friends."
Painful: "At least that didn't happen in front of the boy you really liked."

When we minimize our children's pain, they now have two problems: the original one they brought up, as well as feeling alone and misunderstood.

Often if you stay with their feelings, they will get to the positives of the situation on their own. This isn't easy to do. I had to bite my lip regularly to not jump in and try to fix my children's problems.

Validation with Empathy Has Two Important Parts:

1. Mirroring back to your children what you understand their thoughts and feelings to be.

Mirroring is important with all ages of children, including babies. Mirroring gives children a sense of self.

They get their view of themselves from what we and other significant people in their lives tell them about who and what they are.

They get these messages by how we respond to them verbally and nonverbally.

Here's an example:

Child: [Crying.]
Mom: "You're angry about not being able to go to the park."
Child: "No."
Mom: "You're not?"
Child: "No."
Mom: "Okay. Well, are you feeling bad because we didn't go to the park?"
Child: "Yes."
Mom: "So, you are feeling bad about not going, do you know what else you are feeling?"
Child: "Sad."

Mom: "You're feeling sad. Some kids like you might also feel lonely, or disappointed, or frustrated too. Do you feel any of those things?"

Child: "Lonely. I think Jimmy was going to be there."

Mom: "You feel sad and lonely because we didn't go to the park, and then you missed out on seeing Jimmy?"

Child: "Yes."

Mom: "Oh, that does sound hard. When I don't get to see my friends when I hoped I would, it feels very sad. I'm so sorry this is so hard for you."

Validating your child's feelings doesn't mean you give in and go to the park. It means you feel bad with them for their loss and keep the boundary you already set to not go to the park.

Here's another example:

You're in the grocery store with your kids. They are clamoring for Cocoa Puffs, which you have no intention of buying. Your first instinct is to snap at them and say, *"No! We're not here to buy that. Put that down!"*

What works better is to validate how much they'd like you to buy Cocoa Puffs, without buying them. Before you try this, here's an important tip. I discovered by accident that the key is to never stop the cart for any reason! When you get to the Cocoa Puffs, or whatever else they are clamoring for, you say something like the following.

Mom: "You really like Cocoa Puffs, and you want me to buy them."

Child: "Yes!"

Mom: "What do you like the most about them?"

Child: "Chocolate, crunchy, and there's chocolate milk in the bottom at the end."

Mom: "Yes, they are good. Aren't we glad God made Cocoa Puffs?"

Child: "Yes."

Mom: "We aren't going to get any today, but they do sound yummy."

At this point you are in the next aisle, and they see something else. Let them pick something on your trip that you are fine with. They have two needs in this situation, for you to get how wonderful Cocoa Puffs are and for you to buy them.

By validating the glory of Cocoa Puffs, you've met one of their needs, and they will calm down.

2. If you misunderstand your child's feelings, you correct what you said.

Here's an example:

Child: [Not picking up toys.]

Mom: "It seems like you aren't picking up your toys."

Child: "Not going to."

Mom: "You aren't picking up your toys, so you must not want them anymore."

Child: "NOOOOOOOOOOO… I do want them."

Mom: "Well you must not, or you'd be picking them up."

Child: [Even more distressed. His mom doesn't understand how he's feeling, and now he's in trouble and might lose his toys.] "NOOOOOO!" [Then he starts a tantrum.]

Mom: [Realizes she's missed what was really going on. Scoops him up.] "Oh, I got that wrong. You do want your toys, but you aren't in the mood to pick them up. Let's rest for a minute while you calm down, and then we'll figure out what to do."

A bit later…

Mom: "Before when you weren't picking up your toys I wasn't sure why. Was it because it's hard work and you need help, or you're really tired, or something else?"
Child: "I don't want to. It's too much, I can't do it."
Mom: "How about if we figure out how to not make it so hard."

These types of validating interactions help your children in so many ways:

- They build an understanding relationship between you and your children.
- Your children will feel closer to you, more open to sharing, and safer with you because you understand.
- They will get over their disappointment more quickly, because they don't have to keep escalating their behavior to get you to understand. Sometimes the reason a child's behavior gets worse and worse is because they are so frustrated that you don't get how they are feeling. They then instinctually have to "up the ante" in hopes you will get it.
- They are more likely to cooperate, and not continue to rebel, because they've been able to settle down inside when you understood what they were sharing. This is important across all ages, and especially so with teens.

- When we validate their feelings, they will learn to do this for themselves. If they don't learn how to be kind to themselves when upset, they will always be looking for someone else to validate their feelings. This makes them vulnerable to the whims of others. They may stay in jobs, friendships, or relationships with others that aren't good for them as they try to get others to give them the empathy and validation they need.

What Happens if Emotional Closeness Does Not Occur?

CHILDREN MAY FEEL unloved, unimportant, angry, depressed, and alone. They may act out these painful feelings in behavior problems. Young children may find themselves hitting, dawdling, crying, biting, and refusing to be cooperative as they struggle with built-up feelings inside.

Teenagers may turn to substances or activities to numb the pain and loneliness inside, such as drugs, alcohol, sex, and excessive internet use.

Now What? Where Do I Start?

1. Pray, and ask God for wisdom and help. Ask Him to help you begin to increase the emotional closeness between you and your children. Ask Him to give you wisdom where to start with each child. Also pray for patience and the ability to make needed changes.
2. Realize that we tend to duplicate the level of emotional closeness we grew up with. You may tend to gravitate toward the type of closeness you had growing up, even if you want this to be different in your family now. Think

about how much closeness was in your family of origin. The good news is it's possible to make changes, but it will take concentrated effort.

3. Choose one area that you would like to work on for each child (Eye Contact, Physical Touch, Focused Attention, Validation with Empathy), and give it a try.
4. Speak to yourself with compassion. *"There was a lot in this chapter. It is good to know exactly what helps parents and children achieve a close relationship. I'm doing some of them but not others. I'm tempted to beat myself up for what I'm not doing, but I don't want to. I think I'll focus on empathizing with my children this week and see how it goes. It is a challenge to be a parent, and I don't have to do this perfectly."*

4

Getting Your Kids to Listen

My sheep listen to my voice;
I know them, and they follow me.

John 10:27

ALL PARENTS WANT to be listened to, respected, and taken seriously. It's hard when our children don't listen to us, especially since we have such good things to say! The good news is that there are lots of ways that increase the chances our children will pay attention to what we say.

The Foundation for Getting Your Kids to Listen to You

SO HERE'S THE secret. Having a strong emotional relationship with our kids makes more of a positive difference than any parenting techniques we employ. When children feel emotionally connected to their parents, they feel known and accepted, and they are much more likely to listen.

Emotional connection happens when we spend time together—playing, listening, working together, and accomplishing goals together. There are a lot of things you can do to establish an emotionally close relationship with your child.

As they feel connected to you emotionally, they are more likely to listen to you. Here's a brief recap of the ways I shared in chapter 3 that will help you build a close relationship with your child:

Eye Contact

BABIES AS WELL as small children soak in love through eye contact and being held. Whenever you are interacting with them, make sure you make eye contact both when things are going well and when they are not. Try not to look away or ignore them when they've done something wrong. You don't want to accidentally give them the message that they are unacceptable to look at when they mess up.

Physical Touch

KIDS SOAK UP hugs, kisses, and being held. As children grow they may prefer other ways to connect physically, such as sitting close while watching TV or reading, wrestling, or pats on the shoulder.

Get to know your children and what they like.

Focused Attention

THIS MEANS SPENDING focused time with your child every day, if possible, by interacting with them on activities that they enjoy. You may feel like, *"If I give them any more focused attention I'm going to die!"*

We already give them lots of attention just to keep them alive! We feed them, change their diapers, do the laundry, drive them to events, help with homework, and break up fights, to name a few.

Spending fifteen to twenty minutes a day with each child builds a deep emotional connection with them that will help them listen to you and feel loved by you. Ask your child, *"I'd love to spend twenty minutes with you one-on-one most days. What would you like to do during that time?"*

Validation with Empathy

VALIDATING YOUR CHILDREN's feelings helps them feel known and loved. Validating their feelings doesn't mean you agree with them or see things the same way. The purpose is to let them know you understand what they are going through.

You put yourself in the shoes of your two-year-old, five-year-old, or ten-year-old, and ask yourself, *"What must it be like to be my child in this situation? What would it be like for them to have this happen?"* You then reflect back their thoughts and feelings while still applying boundaries.

Let's say your daughter is very upset that her brother touched her favorite shirt. You're probably thinking, *"How could this be the end of the world to her?"*

But it is.

Because you want to connect with her on a heart level, you say,

Mom: "You are really upset that your brother touched your favorite shirt."

Child: "Yeeeeees!"

Mom: "It is so special to you, and you don't want anyone to touch it."

Child: "Nooooooo."

Mom: "I understand how upset you are, and that you are angry. Even though you are angry, you cannot hit your brother. You will need to tell him you are sorry, and next time something like this happens, come to me and tell me what you are upset about instead of hitting him. I love you very much."

When we let them know we understand what they are feeling, they become less upset and calm down. More important, it builds a close relationship with them.

They understand that *"Mommy and Daddy love me, even when I do something wrong."*

How Does Being Emotionally Connected Help Your Kids Listen?

THERE IS A huge connection.

To your child, being connected emotionally means,

"We're on the same side, and my basic emotional needs are being met. If I'm not connected, I feel controlled by your rules, and I am more likely to spend my energy fighting you and trying to get you to see I'm hurting inside. Listening to you will not be high on my priority list!"

Think about this dynamic in your own life.

When your friend, boss, co-worker, or spouse doesn't listen to you and understand what you are saying, you will be much less likely to listen to them.

We are all the same.

Helping Our Kids Listen to Us

A man of knowledge uses words with restraint, and a man of understanding is even-tempered.

Proverbs 17:27

THIS VERSE IS so wise and such a challenge. There are ways we communicate that make us easier to listen to, as well as harder to listen to.

Being a Parent That's Harder to Listen To

A fool finds no pleasure in understanding, but delights in airing his own opinions.

Proverbs 18:2

- Lecturing: We need to avoid having our "talks" turn into lengthy lectures or sermons. Most of us have grown up with the model that it is okay for parents to lecture or talk without listening to their children. Parents who lecture feel like they had a good talk with their child, but there was no conversation. Often the child on the other end of the lecture will feel like their "talk" was awful. We can learn more about our kids by listening to them than by talking "at them." A child who expects to be yelled at, or who feels disconnected, will not listen to us.
- Not enough closeness: If we don't have a close emotional connection with our kids, they will appease us but not really listen to us. Without enough closeness, kids will either aggress against us, pretend to listen, or ignore us.
- Too busy: If we are too busy to spend time with them, our kids' internal needs won't be met, and they will be less likely to listen to us.

- Dismissing or minimizing their feelings: When we try to talk them out of their feelings, or tell them their feelings are wrong, we are essentially not listening to the tender part of themselves they are trying to share. When we dismiss or minimize their feelings, they won't listen to us.

Mom: "Did you have fun at Amy's house?"
Child: "No, she was mean."
Mom: "No, she's not. You like Amy."
Child: [Louder.] "No I don't. She was mean."
Mom: "She's your best friend!"
Child: [Collapses on floor and throws a fit.]
Mom: "Boy, I don't know what's wrong with you!"

Here's another example:
Dad: "Get your shoes on, we're going to the park."
Child: "I don't want to go to the park today."
Dad: "Yes, you do. You asked me yesterday if we could go."
Child: "Going to the park is stupid."
Dad: "No, it isn't. I can push you on the swings and throw the ball around."
Child: "The park is for losers!"
Dad: "Don't talk that way!"

The child's attempts to share his perceptions, ideas, and feelings are turned into an argument. This happens when we don't stop to listen to what they are trying to tell us. Believe me, I know from experience how frustrating it is as a parent to have these kinds of conversations. Later in the chapter we'll revisit these two scenarios.

It's worth trying to unpack what is really going on inside our struggling children. It will build a solid relationship with them, as well as help your children identify their feelings. If a child's attempts to share her feelings are discounted over time, she will start to distrust herself and instead trust others' beliefs about who she is and how she feels. This may cause her to be vulnerable to the influences of others rather than trust her own gut instincts.

Being a Parent Who's Easier to Listen To

- Listens more than talks: Often our kids may seem like aliens from another planet. We need to listen to find out what is going on in their hearts and minds. As we ask questions, they get to know themselves better too. In order for our kids to listen to us, we need to listen to them.
- Makes time for relationship with kids: Be creative about ways to connect with your kids. We are busy, and it's a challenge to get food on the table, do laundry, go to work, and handle all the details of life. Try to let go of things that are not necessary to make sure you have time to be with and enjoy your kids. Let them know how much you miss them when you have to be gone. Let them know that you are looking forward to spending time with them and then follow through. In our world, we often have way too many activities and way too little time to talk, play, and hang out with our children. I remember when our daughter was five or six. I was going to work, and she said that she would miss me. I replied back how much I would miss her too. This comforted her. She said, *"You will?"* I said, *"Yes, of course. I think about you all day when I'm at work, and I can't wait to get back home to be with you."* I could see her settle down in-

side. I think she assumed that because I was going to work, I didn't miss her.

- Pays more attention to *being* with them than *doing* for them: We often run around doing things for our kids because we love them so much. They benefit from all we do, unless we are so busy we can't spend time playing, talking, and hanging out with them. Our society puts so much pressure to have our kids be involved in everything, and some of these activities can take over our lives. We end up running them from here to there, not having much time with them, while everyone else has a relationship with them. They thrive when we regularly take the time to hang out and find out how they are doing on the inside.
- Listens to and accepts their feelings. "*The purposes of a man's heart are deep waters, but a man of understanding draws them out*" (Proverbs 20:5). This helps them feel understood and loved on the inside. We want them to know that we love and care about their inward self, not just their outward behavior. This will be harder to do if:

    - you haven't been listened to in this way, as a child or an adult;
    - you have a belief that children are to be "seen and not heard";
    - the topic your child is talking about is something that is either very important to you or that scares you; or
    - you place a lot of value on obedience versus relationship.

Ways We Don't Accept Our Children's Feelings

He who answers before
listening—that is his folly and his shame.

Proverbs 18:13

THERE ARE LOTS of ways we don't listen to and accept our children's feelings. Now, don't get down on yourself for this. We usually parrot back to our kids what was said to us when we tried to share our feelings when we were children. If you fall into a few of the categories below, most likely you're responding automatically. Don't worry, we'll learn some new ways to respond to our children's feelings together.

- Denial of their feelings: "You have no reason to be upset. There's nothing to worry about."
- Dismissing child's concerns: "Don't be silly. There's no reason to feel that way…"
- Shutting down discussion: "Oh, you don't really mean that. I don't want to hear that talk."
- Being matter-of-fact: "That happens to everyone. No friend is perfect."
- Giving Advice: "Here's what you should do…you go and tell your friend that she is being selfish. If you do what I tell you, you won't have this problem."
- Minimizing: "It wasn't that bad. It could have been so much worse."
- Looking on the bright side: "Don't worry, be happy. It will be okay."

These types of responses cause your child to close down inside. In contrast, when someone is willing to really listen to our inner hurt and give us the time to talk about what happened, we usually calm down and are able to come up with our own solutions.

HELPFUL WAYS TO RESPOND TO OUR CHILDREN'S FEELINGS

LISTENING WITH EMPATHY

WE SOMETIMES PUSH away our child's unhappy feelings because we want them to be happy. Unfortunately, this doesn't help. They need us to help them with their feelings, otherwise they become stuck in them. The easier it is for us to listen to and accept their painful feelings, the easier it is for them to let go of them.

This type of listening and responding is different from just listening for the content of what is being said. When we listen empathetically, we also listen for the emotions that are present. We do this by watching for the following.

- The child's body language, facial expressions, and gestures.
- The child's perspective. What would it be like to be this age child in this situation, with this family life, with this age skills?
- The child's state of heart. We use our own hearts to feel what the child is feeling.

"Boy, that sounds really hard. You studied so hard for that test and gave it your all. You sound shocked and discouraged by your grade. I'm so sorry you are going through this. We'll figure out later what to do. For now, I want you to know how sorry I am that this happened."

When your child opens up her heart, she gives you the gift of sharing her internal world, which is precious. We return this gift by mirroring back to our child both what she is saying and feeling.

TIPS TO EMPATHETICALLY CONNECT WITH YOUR CHILD:

- Calm yourself first. If you aren't relatively calm, take a deep breath and ask God for help. Keep in mind this is more than just the incident at hand. This is a time to teach about emotions and build closeness and safety between you and your child.
- With younger children, sit at their level. Older children may open up while talking in the car, sitting on the couch, or doing a common task together. Focus on your child, and don't do two things at once. Your child will pick up your body language, so try to approach your child in as open a position as possible.
- Listen for both the thoughts and feelings being expressed, and reflect back to your child what you are hearing and seeing. It is better to reflect on what you notice, *"You looked away when I said we'd need to leave soon,"* rather than ask kids why questions or tell them what they are feeling.
- Help your child label his or her emotions using words. Kids can usually tell they are feeling uncomfortable emotions, but they might not be able to label them as jealousy, frustration, worry, sadness, or anxiety. It helps them to know it is normal, and even common, to feel more than one feeling at once.
- Don't jump into problem-solving, correction, or lecturing. We may feel like we are handling the situation, but we aren't. While it is understandable to jump in and focus on

the facts, it is not helpful to the larger goal of establishing a safe emotional relationship with your child. When we immediately correct or give a simple solution, it shuts down a concern that is serious for our child, and gives a message that our child's problems are silly and inconsequential.

HELP THEM WITH THEIR EMOTIONS

WHEN WE HELP our children understand their emotions, they will feel less overwhelmed and out of control. It also helps them ac-cept those emotions. It isn't wrong to feel angry, jealous, sad, or frustrated. It's part of everyday life. As we label emotions, the following happens.

- It helps us understand and have compassion for what they are going through. "You're feeling disappointed that things didn't work out with your friend. That is so hard."
- It also helps your child feel understood and loved. When we are feeling crummy, usually the only thing that takes the edge off the pain is knowing that someone loves you and feels bad with you.
- It gives your child an experience of being soothed when upset emotionally. This in turn helps your child to learn how to self-soothe when in emotional pain. There is no way to describe how important this skill is for living life.
- Being able to self-soothe helps one to:
    - not fall into addictions in order to numb or soothe internal pain;
    - calm oneself when upset, thus reducing the chance of impulsive choices and decisions;
    - concentrate better, and therefore learn better;
    - have better friendships; and

- have better health, because emotional pain is not being stored in the body.

LISTENING AND CONNECTING WITH YOUR CHILDREN HELPS THEM LISTEN TO YOU

AS WE MAKE time to bond with our children and listen to them, they will listen to us. John 10:27 tells us, *"My sheep listen to my voice; I know them, and they follow me."*

This verse is full of wisdom for us. Jesus had just shared the parable of the Good Shepherd. He shared that the reason His followers listened to Him is because He knows them and they follow Him.

Notice what is first. He knows them. They follow Him.

This is where we need to focus, on knowing them rather than trying to force them to listen to us. That never works. As we deepen our relationship with our child and get to know them internally the best we can, there is a greater chance they will listen to what we have to share.

Let's put all we've learned in this chapter together, by revisiting the two scenarios shared at the beginning of the chapter.

Mom: "Did you have fun at Amy's house?"
Child: "No, she was mean."
Mom: "She was?"
Child: "Yeah." [Head down and a little teary.]
Mom: "I'm so sorry. It sounds like something hard must have happened."
Child: "Yeah." [Crying a little more.]
Mom: "Come sit with me. I want to hear all about it. What happened?"

Child: "Ann was there too, and Ann and Amy ended up playing together, and they left me in the other room. I asked why, and Ann said, 'Only girls whose names start with 'A' could play.'"

Mom: "Oh no. That must have been so hard. You are very sad this happened. What else did you feel like?"

Child: "Mixed up, I didn't know what was happening."

Mom: "I'll bet that was very confusing. Were there any other feelings too? Maybe angry or lonely or something else?"

Child: "Lonely. I felt all alone, and I didn't know what to do." [Crying some more.]

Mom: "That was so hard. You went for a fun time with your friend Amy and instead it was really hard, and you felt sad, confused, and all alone. What did Amy do when Ann said that?"

Child: "She looked at me kind of sad. Then Ann took her by the hand and pulled her into the other room. I don't think she knew what to do either."

Mom: "That makes sense. Ann sounds pretty bossy. It sounds like Ann was mean, and Amy went along with it because she didn't know what to do."

Child: "Yeah, I think so."

Mom: "Well I'm so very sorry that happened. You are a wonderful friend, and you and Amy have always had fun playing together. Maybe you could tell yourself, 'I'm a very nice girl and a good friend. I had a really hard day. It makes sense I feel bad. I'll feel better soon.' Is that okay to say to yourself?"

Child: "Yes."

Mom: "Anything else?"

Child: "I'm not going to play with Amy if Ann is there."

Mom: "I'm so glad you told me what happened. Is there anything else I can do to help?"

Child: "No. Thanks, Mommy."

Notice how much more information this little girl shared with her mom. As her mom listened, empathized, and labeled her feelings, her daughter opened up more and calmed down. Her mom was able to point out that maybe Amy didn't know what to do either, and shared a way that her daughter could be compassionate with herself. A side benefit is that her daughter problem solved on her own to not put herself in that situation in the future.

This mom may want to revisit this topic later and talk about what her daughter could do differently next time or how she'll handle it next time she plays with Amy. Her daughter will be much more open to what her mom shares to help her daughter develop skills to deal with difficult situations in the future.

Compassion for the Mom in This Situation

THIS MOM ASKED her daughter a simple question and expected a simple answer. She was probably on her way to put in a load of laundry, return calls for work, or take a break after a long day. All that came to a standstill when she decided to listen to her daughter share about her painful moment with a friend.

What a hard spot to be in. She had many responsibilities to attend to, and she also wanted to tend to her child's sad heart. She, no doubt, had to take a deep breath inside and say to herself, *"She is so sad. Something bad must have happened. Part of me wants to treat her comment lightly and get to the chores I still have to do before my head hits the pillow. Those are important, and so is her little heart. God, please help me calm down and take the time to find out what happened. Please give me the words to say."*

Afterwards, I'd encourage this mom to say something like this to herself, *"Boy, that was hard. I wasn't ready for that. I'm pleased I was able to calm myself down and really listen to how she was doing. I'm so glad she was able to tell me what happened. We both felt so much closer to one another after our talk. I can think of other things I wished I'd said, but all in all, I did a good job. Hopefully this will be one of many times I'm able to really listen and empathize with my sweet daughter."*

Let's go back and revisit this dad, as he takes time to find out what's going on with his son.

Dad: "Get your shoes on, we're going to the park."
Child: "I don't want to go to the park today."
Dad: "You don't? You asked me yesterday if we could go."
Child: "Going to the park is stupid."
Dad: "Really? It seemed like you really wanted to go yesterday. What happened?"
Child: "I just don't want to go."
Dad: "Come on over and hang with me for a bit."
Child: [Sits by Dad and looks sad.] "I told Jimmy we were going to go to the park today, and he laughed at me and said the park was for losers."
Dad: "Oh, so then you decided you didn't want to go to the park today? You look pretty sad."
Child: [Crying a little.] "I am. I really do want to go to the park today with you. I like it when we go together."
Dad: "I like it too. Sounds like you don't want Jimmy to think you're a loser. You want him to be your friend. Is that right?"
Child: "Yeah."
Dad: "I'm so sorry that happened. It seems really hard, and you probably didn't know what to say. Besides feel-

ing sad, I wonder if you might be feeling stuck. You want to go to the park with me, and you don't want Jimmy to think you're a loser. It's hard to know what to do."

Child: "Yeah, it really is."

Dad: "Do you know if Jimmy goes to the park or does stuff with his dad?"

Child: "His parents are divorced. He hardly ever sees his dad."

Dad: "I wonder if it was hard to know that you were going to get to go to the park with your dad, when he isn't able to spend time with his dad? What do you think?"

Child: "Maybe…I never thought of that."

Dad: "That's something we all do. It hurts to think of things we don't get to do, so we say they're stupid or for losers. Maybe that's what Jimmy was trying to do. Does Jimmy say other things to you that make you sad?"

Child: "No, he's usually so nice. I was surprised he said that. I didn't know what to do. Maybe I just shouldn't tell him when we are going to do fun things together. I don't want to make him feel bad."

Dad: "That's a possibility, although it might feel bad to you to not be able to be yourself with Jimmy. Do you think there's any way we could include Jimmy in some of the times you and I hang out?"

Child: "Yeah! Really? That would be fun. Can I call him right now?"

Dad: "Sure. I'll want to talk with his mom too, just to give her details of where we're going. I won't say anything about him saying the park is for losers. If he can't come today, you can invite him for next time."

Child: "Thanks, Dad! I don't feel sad anymore."

Compassion for This Dad

WHAT A GREAT job this dad did. It would have been normal for him to be angry and irritated with his son. His son asked him to go to the park together the day before, and he went out of his way to make this happen.

There were lots of other things this dad could have been doing with his time.

He noticed that his son responded differently than normal, and he wanted to find out what was going on. He calmed himself emotionally and asked his son to sit next to him while he gently probed what was going on.

Once he figured out what was going on, he helped his son identify his feelings, empathized with him, and helped him see how Jimmy was hurting too. Out of this came a possible solution that was good for all.

Afterwards, I'd encourage this dad to say something like this to himself, *"Whew, I'm glad that turned out okay. I sure didn't expect him to say he didn't want to go to the park. I almost yelled at him. I'm so glad I didn't. It is sure hard to be a good parent sometimes. I could tell something was wrong, he looked so sad. I'm pleased I could have compassion for him and also help him see that Jimmy was hurting inside. I did a good job with my son today."*

You love your children. You have so much wisdom to share with them that will improve their lives. It is so normal that you want your children to listen to what you have to share. As you deepen your relationships with your children, there will be many benefits to you and your family.

Don't forget to be compassionate with yourself about where you struggle.

NOW WHAT? WHERE DO I START?

1. Pray. Ask God for wisdom and help to discern where you need to begin. Is it in stopping certain ways of responding to your children/teens? Is it in increasing your time together? Is it in the area of listening with empathy?

2. Ask yourself some important questions:

    - Do I make it harder or easier for my child to listen to me?
    - What gets in the way of listening to my child?
    - Were my feelings listened to as a child?
    - What is one thing I can try this week?

3. Choose one area you would like to focus on for each child:

    - Eye contact
    - Physical touch
    - Focused attention
    - Validation with empathy
    - Listening to them

4. Come up with a plan for how you might implement these ideas, and start!

5. Speak to yourself with compassion. *"I never realized how the way I listen, respond, and connect to my children affects whether they listen to me or not. Yesterday I yelled and slammed a door because I was so frustrated with my kids. I feel bad about this. I don't*

want to yell at them. Rather than beat myself up or eat a quart of ice cream, I think I'll be kind to myself. No one has ever taught me this important information before. I can learn, and I can start today. I think I'm going to try listening to them more, and I'll give them my undivided attention, even if only for ten minutes. I feel hopeful that being compassionate to myself and to my kids will help."

5

Healthy Boundaries: Setting Limits with Love

Carry each other's burdens, and in this way, you will fulfill the law of Christ. If anyone thinks they are something when they are not, they deceive themselves. Each one should test their own actions. Then they can take pride in themselves alone, without comparing themselves to someone else, for each one should carry their own load.

Galatians 6:2–5

IT'S NOT EASY to find the sweet spot of setting limits and boundaries without accidentally shaming our kids. In this chapter, we'll examine why setting limits with love is so important for our children's future, as well as a compassionate relationship with themselves.

CHILD DEVELOPMENT 101

SIMPLY PUT, CHILDREN come out as a "blob." They are wonderful creations made by God, but they don't know anything about anything. They know nothing about boundaries or right from wrong.

As far as they know, everything is all good. They want what they want, and they want it now. There is no one else to consider but themselves. Boundaries are a rude awakening for them. This perspective is normal when they are little. Remembering these truths will help us have compassion for our kids.

When children are born, they have no internal sense of what's right and wrong. As parents, we set external boundaries for them to follow so they know what's okay and not okay. It takes thousands of repetitions over time for them to develop their own internal conscience to guide them to do what is right in how they treat others and themselves.

We want them to be able to tell themselves, *"I really want to cheat on that test, but I won't because it's wrong."* Or *"I want to cheat on this test, but I won't because if I get caught I'll get suspended."*

We want to teach our children boundaries with love and not with shame. We don't want them to feel shame inside when corrected. Shame says, *"I am a bad person,"* rather than *"what I did was wrong."* We want to share boundaries with love and not shame. When we set boundaries, we want them to come away with the idea that, *"That was wrong for me to do, but I'm still a good person, and Mommy and Daddy still loves me."*

The truth is they are not bad. They're little kids who are learning difficult lessons about right and wrong. We want them to come away with, *"I was supposed to do my chores and I didn't, so now I can't watch my favorite show"* versus *"I didn't do my chores, and now I'm a bad person."*

When we set healthy boundaries, we want the consequences to teach them about reality. We don't want shame to cause internal self-hatred.

THREE MAIN WAYS TO TEACH BOUNDARIES

1. Teaching – The first one is through teaching. For instance, *"If you hit your brother you'll have to sit for a time-out,"* or *"If you hit your brother, you'll have to do his chores this week."*
2. Modeling – Kids learn from watching what we do. We are their primary models for setting boundaries and handling life. They observe how we handle frustrations, get along with others, and solve problems. They watch how we take care of ourselves, the language we use, and the way we drive. They watch to see how we handle the daily responsibilities of life. It causes confusion when we tell them, *"you need follow-through," "clean your room,"* or *"share with your sister,"* but don't follow through ourselves. They experience an internal conflict when we say one thing but do another.
3. Experience – As we follow through on our consequences, they will internalize reality. They need to feel the reality that when they don't clear their dishes, they don't get dessert.

TEACH THEM REALITY

Do not be deceived, God is not mocked; for whatever a man sows, that he will also reap.

Galatians 6:7 (NKJV)

WE REAP WHAT WE SOW

THEY NEED US to teach them that actions have natural consequences. This is how life works. We need to give them an environment of reality. If "A" happens, then "B" happens. Without meaning to, we may jump in and rescue our kids from the natural consequences they need to experience in order to learn from their mistakes.

If we are too fuzzy with our boundaries, they will go into the world and expect other people to be lax with them too. Sometimes parents put up with behavior that no one in their future life will put up with. Teaching them reality gently will help them to be able to go out into the world, live with societal rules, and be successful in life.

God understands. It is easy to feel overwhelmed with the task of teaching your children responsibility. Ask Him for his help, wisdom, and resources as you continue to teach your children responsibility.

We Need to See the Big Picture

No discipline seems pleasant at the time,
but painful. Later on, however, it produces a
harvest of righteousness and peace for those who
have been trained by it.

Hebrews 12:11

IT'S HARD TO discipline our children. We love them and don't want them to be unhappy or mad at us. What helped me stay consistent was reminding myself of the big picture. I parented with my children's long-term character development in mind. If we just look at the moment, we may not understand that the boundary we are enforcing is about developing our child's character.

The boundary I'm setting at age two is about preparing my child for his teenager years. I want him to learn self-control over many years so he is ready to handle peer pressure when it comes. Making sure my daughter cleans up her room is about helping her complete unwanted responsibilities so she can have a successful career and relationships.

With every boundary, I realize I am shaping their character, which will determine the future of their lives.

When our son just turned two, he was trying out disobeying. His baby sister was six months old, and he decided he really wanted her toys, even though he knew he shouldn't take them. I told him that I understood that he wanted her toys, but he could not take them from her. If he did, he would get a time-out.

Of course, he kept taking them. I followed through by telling him why this was wrong, and I put him on a short time-out each time it happened. I remember thinking after the third time-out that this could really get out of hand if I didn't keep on top of it.

I didn't see him as a rebellious child. I saw him as a two-year-old who was developing his sense of self and realized he wanted some things. Parents often misunderstand what the "terrible twos" are all about. It is easy to see your child as bad or selfish, but it isn't this at all.

About eighteen months, they start having their own ideas and preferences. Little kids first learn to say what they don't want, "no," before saying what they do want.

Our son learned that he couldn't take his sister's toys without experiencing a negative consequence himself. This was the beginning of developing self-control, delayed gratification, and being kind to others.

It may strike you as a lot of work to apply boundaries and limits in a consistent way. The truth is, it is. I always reminded myself that I could "pay now" by consistently setting boundaries and applying consequences, or "pay later" with a child a few years older who was out of control. The price tag is smaller when they are young.

Reality Consequences vs. Relational Consequences

THERE ARE TWO types of consequences we need to look at. We get into big trouble when we don't distinguish between the two:

- Reality Consequences – Negative behavior results in real-life consequences such as incurring a time-out or losing allowance, privileges, possessions, things we enjoy, and people we value.
- Relational Consequences – Negative behavior results in nagging, getting angry, giving the silent treatment, or trying to manipulate us through guilt or shame.

Life works on reality consequences. True change usually only occurs when we receive these types of consequences. Negative relational consequences may produce short-term compliance, but it won't produce long-term learning or internal character growth. A child might do her chores because of unwanted relational consequences such as her mom yelling and nagging her. This is in contrast to doing chores because it's the right thing to do, or because she doesn't want to lose allowance to pay a sibling to do the chores she forgot.

Where We Tend to Goof Up

LET'S BE HONEST, it isn't easy to set boundaries. It is a challenge to set them and follow through. Here are the reasons most of us find it hard to set boundaries and follow through with consequences.

- **We see setting boundaries as uncaring.**

Some of us may refuse to allow our kids to fail because we see such a response as uncaring. We jump in and rescue them, but doing so is actually uncaring, because we take away the opportunity for them to solve their own problems and learn from their mistakes. It's as if we think we can help our kids avoid the tough situations in life.

Well, you know what? That is impossible. Hard things do happen. If we parent so our kids are "happy," they will go out into the world, have a lot of hard things happen, and they won't know how to handle them.

Some good questions to ask yourself: *Do I see setting a boundary with my child as uncaring? Do I think I can step in and save my children from the difficulties of life?*

- **We may not realize the danger done to children's character and future when boundaries aren't set.**

Not consistently enforcing boundaries with our children is dangerous to them. As a counselor, I often helped parents of college-age children who were struggling. I noticed that some of these college students did not experience many boundaries and consequences when they were children. They'd go off to college and fall apart, because they hadn't developed their own internal boundaries of acceptable behavior. They had problems with alcohol, going to class, and finishing their semester. Often, their parents had to pick them up halfway through the semester.

They either dropped out of school completely or went to a community college and lived at home. They couldn't handle the freedom of college life because they didn't have internal boundaries to guide their own behavior.

We need to remind ourselves that the boundaries we set now will help them develop strong character. This will help them live a successful life later. Some good questions to ask yourself: *Is my hesitancy to set boundaries stopping my children from developing a strong character? Are they learning to delay gratification, do the hard things of life, and make good choices?*

- **We tend to think that telling our kids to be responsible works.**

It doesn't. Children primarily learn through consequences. Telling them to do the right thing seldom does. They need to experience real-life consequences to learn and grow.

A good question to ask yourself: *Do I think that if I tell my kids to do the right thing they will do so without having painful experiences?*

- **We don't want our kids to be mad at us.**

We may as well forget that one! If your kids are never mad at you, that means you aren't setting boundaries and teaching them right from wrong.

If it is really painful when your child is mad at you, you may have some unresolved pain inside regarding times others were mad at you. If this is the case, work through your past hurt with a counselor so you can apply boundaries with your kids.

Some good questions to ask yourself: *Does it cause me distress when my child is mad at me? Do I cave in rather than risking my child being mad at me? When my child is mad, does it bring up pain from the past?*

- **We depend on our child for emotional closeness.**

If we don't have enough healthy nurturing relationships with adults in our life, we may find it hard to set boundaries with our child. It may feel too painful for us to endure our child's anger, distance or disapproval of us.

A good question to ask yourself: *"Am I afraid that if I say no to my child, that I can't handle her being distant?"*

- **We over identify with our child's feelings and struggles.**

It is very important to understand and empathize with our children's feelings. Where we get into trouble, is when we confuse their painful feelings with our own. This is especially true when we have similar unresolved emotions inside of us. When this happens, we may think the child is in more trouble than he is, because we are feeling not only the child's current pain, but also our own built up pain. A mother who has unresolved issues may see her child's distress as a crisis. A father who struggles with anger may see his son's normal frustration as rage.

Some good questions to ask yourself: *"What emotions does my child feel that tap into my own pain of the past? Is it possible I overreact to normal struggles because of my own unresolved emotional pain?"*

- **We ignore misbehavior.**

This happens when we put up with bad behavior, hoping it will go away. Instead, the bad behavior gets worse, and resentment grows. Finally, we LOSE IT! We tend to use this approach if we hate conflict, believe that problems will go away on their own, or have never had any training on how to discipline with grace and truth.

Generally, problems that are not dealt with get worse not better. Ignoring misbehavior teaches children that they can breaks the limits over and over until mom or dad "loses it." Then they just have to endure the anger and yelling until it's over.

Some good questions to ask yourself: *"Do I ignore problems hoping they will just go away? How does this actually work? Is my child learning to not hear me, or ignore me?"*

- **We are too worn down to follow through with discipline.**

Kids are human and would rather take the easy way if they can. They will often put a lot of energy into avoiding a responsibility, and don't give up easily. When we are worn down, we are even more susceptible to giving up our boundaries to avoid a fight.

We get worn down for a variety of reasons. We may be exhausted by the demands of life and don't have enough replenishing relationships and/or activities in our lives. We may have accidentally trained our kids to just keep pushing until we give in.

Being worn down makes it harder to set limits and enforce consequences.

Some good questions to ask yourself: *"Am I so overloaded that I find it difficult to set limits and consequences? Deep down do I think that if I ignore a bad behavior it will just go away?*

- **We have a strong need to be in control.**

If this is the case, we may not let our children fail, so they can learn from their mistakes. We may feel uncomfortable watching our children learn from trial and error, so may not allow them the process of learning on their own. If we lower our anxiety by having things under control, we may step in to orchestrate things, rather than giving our children both the freedom to fail, and to learn things on their own.

Some good questions to ask: *"Do I step in to tell my child the 'right' way to do things rather than letting them figure it out for themselves? Do others tell me I'm controlling or a control freak?*

Do I become uncomfortable when my children want to discover things themselves or have different desires and plans than I?"

YOUR CHILDREN'S JOB

THE REALITY IS that our children's job is to test our resolve so they can learn about reality. They don't know what reality is like. It's like they are in a maze, trying different things to see what works and what doesn't.

They aren't usually trying to do the wrong thing. They rely on us to give them a picture of how the world works.

YOUR JOB

YOUR JOB IS to withstand the tests and not take the pushing of your boundaries personally. This means knowing your limits, stating the boundaries and consequences clearly, and standing firm to apply logical consequences.

Part of the job is to not be surprised when our precious children pout, throw a tantrum, are angry with us, or turn away.

We give them a gift when we endure their displeasure with us so they will learn how to be successful, functional adults someday.

Nobody's perfect.

It's better to shoot for being consistent overall. Nobody's consistent every day. I'm not.

It's okay to apologize when we're wrong, because that's how our kids will learn to do this too.

More on this in chapter 6, "Parenting with Grace and Truth: Building Personal Responsibility"

Tips for Setting Boundaries

- Don't forget the love, empathy, and validation. Setting boundaries is so much easier when we have the attitude that we are teaching and guiding our children rather than punishing them.
- Make sure the consequence fits the crime.
- Make sure you use "reality consequences," not shame, guilt, or anger.
- The younger the child, the more immediate the consequence.

  With very small kids…
    - Say no firmly.
    - Use time-outs.
    - Remove them from the situation.
    - Put the toy in time-out.

  With older kids…
    - If they're late for dinner, they might miss dinner.
    - A story will be available at 7:30 to all who have their PJs on and teeth brushed.
    - I'm happy to get you school supplies with twenty-four-hours' notice, otherwise you'll have to be creative and make do.
    - If chores are not completed by 5:00 p.m. on Saturday, some of your allowance will be used to pay your sister to do your chores.
    - Snack will be available after you put your blocks away.

- Giving extra understanding when children are going through a special circumstance, such as parents' divorce, separation, new baby, or a parent or child illness. This doesn't mean you let things go. It means you show them compassion by acknowledging the hard time they are going through, giving them extra time and attention, and helping them follow through.

Learning to set clear boundaries is a very important part of parenting. How we establish and enforce these boundaries also makes a huge difference. It's not too late to start setting consistent boundaries with your children. We'll learn more in the next chapter about helping our kids become responsible by balancing grace and truth.

Now What? Where Do I Start?

1. Ask God for help. You don't have to do this alone. Ask Him to help you figure out which boundaries to set this week.
2. Do you tend to use relational consequences or reality consequences?
3. For extra help, read "Boundaries with Kids" by Henry Cloud and John Townsend.
4. What stops you from setting boundaries?
    - I tend to see setting boundaries as uncaring.
    - I didn't realize how not setting boundaries could hurt my children.
    - I thought if I told them to be responsible it would be enough.
    - I don't want my kids to be mad at me.
    - I depend on my children for emotional closeness, so I don't want to risk distance between us.
    - I over identify with my children's feelings and struggles.

- I ignore misbehavior, hoping it will go away on its own.
- I'm too tired to set boundaries.
- I need to be in control.

5. Speak to yourself with compassion. *"I can see how important it is to set consistent boundaries with my children. I realize I'm so busy and exhausted, I don't have the energy to implement them. I feel like I know what to do, which is good, but I am just too exhausted. I think I'll adjust my schedule and drop a few things so I get more rest for myself and have the energy to set the boundaries I want to. Just because I haven't been setting boundaries consistently doesn't mean I'm bad, it just means I'm too busy. I guess I need to set boundaries with myself and others too."*

6

Parenting with Grace and Truth: Building Personal Responsibility

The Word became flesh and made his dwelling among us. We have seen his glory, the glory of the one and only Son, who came from the Father, full of grace and truth.

John 1:14

WE WANT RESPONSIBLE KIDS!

WE ALL WANT to raise kids who are equipped for the challenges of the real world. We deeply desire that they act in ways that are respectful of themselves and others, as well as accept the consequences of their actions or inactions.

We know that personal responsibility will help them negotiate life, be a contributing member of society, and reflect God's love. To accomplish this goal, we need to parent with our child's long-term character development in mind. We don't want them to suffer the rest of their lives because they haven't learned to be responsible.

What will help us accomplish this lofty goal? Parenting with compassion, which is a balance of grace and truth. This way of parenting is so worth the effort.

Parenting with grace means giving kids lots of love and affection, as well as understanding and accepting of their humanness and imperfections. Grace seeks to understand what your child is going through and help them navigate the uncertainties of life. Parents relate with grace when they approach their children with kindness, compassion, and practical help.

Parenting with truth means being clear about what is expected of your child and helping them grow in undeveloped areas. Parents live out truth when they set clear boundaries and follow through with promises and consequences. This lets children know where they stand and gives them a sense of stability.

Our Parenting Style Needs to Include Both Grace and Truth

> *And the Word became flesh and dwelt among us, and we beheld His glory, the glory as of the only begotten of the Father, full of grace and truth. John bore witness of Him and cried out saying, "This was He of whom I said, 'He who comes after me is preferred before me, for He was before me.'"*
>
> *And of His fullness we have all received, and grace for grace. For the law was given through Moses, but grace and truth came through Jesus Christ. No one has seen God at any time. The only begotten Son, who is in the bosom of the Father, He has declared Him.*
>
> John 1:14–18

JESUS IS OUR model, and He is described as being full of grace and truth. In order to be effective, we need to parent with a healthy balance of grace and truth, or there will be problems. Sometimes, without even knowing it, we parent in ways that go against this needed balance of grace and truth. There are four possible combinations of grace (love, warmth, understanding, support, and affection) and truth (consistent rules and consequences):

1. High Grace, Low Truth = Permissive Parenting

THIS STYLE IS high on giving love, warmth, support, and affection. This style is low on truth and has difficulty taking a firm stance and consistently applying consequences when needed.

Parents have difficulty setting clear expectations and consequences for their children's behavior. They feel disempowered, and they may try to get kids to behave through bargaining and pleading. Kids may become bossy with peers and angry and demanding with adults, because they may not know where the limits really are. They may conclude that rules are not meant for them to follow.

We can accidentally fall into telling (translation: nagging, lecturing, threatening, using guilt, or yelling) our kids to be responsible, but that doesn't work. The only thing that actually works are consequences. They end up learning, *"I just need to suffer through the lecture and do what I want. Mom and Dad won't actually apply any consequences."*

When children go through normal difficulties, permissive parents are tempted to rescue their children. They may try to protect their children from discomfort by bringing forgotten lunches, jackets, or homework to school. In addition, parents may step in to protect them from the natural consequences of their actions with teachers, peers, or the law.

While their motivation is good, the results are damaging. These children are unprepared to deal with real life. The real world doesn't have people who will bail us out of traffic tickets, overdue bills, or the hardships of life. The underlying message these kids get is, *"You can't handle life without me to bail you out."*

2. Low Grace, High Truth = Authoritarian Parenting

THIS STYLE IS high on giving expectations about what behavior is acceptable and unacceptable. Rules are clear and the consequences for violating them are consistently enforced.

These parents dearly love their children, but they focus on showing that love by making them "well-disciplined." These kids are not encouraged to think for themselves, and instead are told what to think. Parents with this style focus on outward compliance rather than internal character growth.

This style is low on love, warmth, understanding, support, and affection. Without enough grace and love, kids will not share their real vulnerable self with their parents. Kids may keep others at a distance as they become self-sufficient, but they won't feel deeply loved. Kids will obey and achieve, but they will struggle with anxiety because they haven't received enough love and grace to balance the rules.

This type of parenting stops kids from developing an internal locus of control, which prompts kids to make the right decision because it is the right thing to do. They are motivated internally to make good decisions, rather than externally by parents to do the right thing.

When parents exert high control, children won't fully develop their own conscience, standards, and boundaries. This can have tragic results as they grow up. Children become used to hearing an external voice tell them what to do, rather than their conscience. This leaves them vulnerable to peer groups and to peer pressure. When they start dating and eventually marry, they may be drawn to those who will try to control them.

These children may also rebel in an attempt to finally make their own decisions. They often make poor choices because they haven't had practice to think on their own and make good choices, as well as suffer the consequences. In general, the more controlling we are, the more rebellious they will become.

The underlying message these kids get is, *"You can't think or reason for yourself, so I will do it for you."*

3. Low Grace, Low Truth = Disengaged/Dismissive Parenting

THIS STYLE IS low on both grace (love, warmth, understanding, support, and affection) and truth (consistent rules and consequences). This is the least effective and most damaging type of parenting. Parents are generally uninvolved with their kids, and they may give the following message verbally or nonverbally: *"Go away, leave me alone."* These kids are left to basically raise themselves.

Kids feel rejected, abandoned, and have a lack of worth. They conclude, *"I'm not worth the time. Other things are more important than I am."* They learn to not make waves, and they become "invisible." These kids have trouble trusting, becoming close to others, and developing a sense of who they are as a person. They don't feel loved, and they aren't equipped to handle the realities of life.

4. High Grace, High Truth = Authoritative Parenting

THIS IS THE healthiest style of parenting. It combines firm, consistent discipline with nurturing care. These parents are warm and loving, and they openly express affection. High expectations for responsible and mature behavior are clear. Parents are loving, consistent, and willing to listen to their children. They are also willing to apply logical consequences as needed.

As children grow, parents act as advisors about how life works. The younger the child, the more guidance he needs. As children get older, more and more control and decisions are handed over to the child.

These parents let their children know, *"I'm sure you'll do the right thing, and if you don't, you'll learn something from the experience."*

They want their children to become skilled in handling life so that when they leave home they will be successful. Parents help them learn about life by giving them permission to fail and learn from their mistakes, and they ask their kids lots of questions to help them think through situations and make their own decisions.

Please note that perfection is not necessary, for children or their parents! Children parented in this way feel loved and secure, and at the same time they know what is acceptable behavior. Parents have high expectations for responsible behavior and readily express their love.

PARENTING WITH GRACE AND TRUTH

THERE IS NO guarantee that even if we parent with grace and truth, our kids will turn out responsible and mature. There are always factors such as genetics, mental illness, addiction, and abuse that plays into their development.

The good news is that there are lots of things we can do that will increase the chance that they will become mature and responsible. See chapter 13 for more about this.

Expressing Truth

THE WAY CHILDREN learn to become responsible is by allowing them to fail so they can learn from their mistakes.

God first modeled this strategy to us with Adam and Eve (Genesis 2:16; 3:11, 16–24). He gave them the freedom to make choices, and He let them experience the result of those choices. He set the parameters by informing them ahead of time what the consequences would be.

It was okay for Adam and Eve to eat anything in the garden except from the Tree of Knowledge. They did it anyway and got thrown out of the Garden of Eden. Sin entered the world, life became much more difficult, and their relationship with God was broken. He did not approve of their disobedience, but He loved them enough to let them make their own decision and live with the consequences.

He let reality do the teaching, as opposed to rescuing them or lecturing them, which never works long-term. God understands that we feel overwhelmed with the task of teaching our children responsibility, especially when they don't want to learn it! God is our parent, and He goes through this with us billions of times a day! He will help us as we ask for His help.

One of the greatest gifts we can give our kids is to try to replicate what life will be like in the real world when they grow up. This means allowing and/or creating logical consequences for their behaviors. They need to experience how the real world works, where there are no mommies or daddies to remind them of their responsibilities. In the real world, if they don't do what is expected of them, they will lose their job or fail at their relationships.

The younger the children, the more direction they will need. As they grow, though, we want them to learn from their mistakes early on. A small example of this is when our daughter asked me:

Daughter: "Can you help me remember a deadline for school?"

Me: "No, but you can. What would be a good way to help you remember?"

Daughter: "Write myself a note."

Me: "Where would you like to put the note so you see it?"

Daughter: "At the table where I sit."

Me: "Great!"

If I had said yes, it would have made me responsible, not her. I need to be responsible for me, and she needs to be responsible for her. To protect them from the consequences of their behavior—by rescuing them, not letting them make decisions for themselves (even if they're wrong), or not applying consequences—creates a child who is not ready to live in the real world.

The younger they learn, the less of a price they will pay. We need to allow kids to fail so they can learn from consequences like staying after school or getting a bad grade, which aren't a big deal. The cost for each learning experience goes up with the child's age. The older the child gets, the bigger the decisions and the graver the consequences. We don't want them to start learning when they are starting to drive, date, or get a job.

Part of the way children mature is by learning to think for themselves. If kids are constantly told what to do, they will rebel against us—not necessarily because they are rebellious but because they are not being allowed to think and experience things for themselves. This goes against the normal process God created inside to become independent.

The more controlling we are, the more lost they will be. They will either find someone to tell them what to do, because they don't believe in themselves, or they will become rebellious and controlling themselves.

Expressing Grace and Compassion

THERE ARE MANY ways to relate to our children with grace and compassion:

- Showering them with love and affection. They need concrete ways of soaking in our love. Our love can be expressed through physical affection, kind words, listening, and time spent together.
- Being understanding and accepting of their imperfections. We bestow the gift of grace to our children when we take the time to listen to them and understand what they are going through. We help them understand that learning about life is a process that involves lots of mistakes, and this is okay.
- Correcting their behavior without shame. Without meaning to, we can respond to our children in shaming ways. Shame is not simply a sense that you've done something wrong, it is a sense that something is wrong with you as a person. We can avoid shaming messages by commenting on the behavior we are unhappy with, as opposed to labeling our child as bad.

Here's an example:

Your son hits his friend when he is frustrated.

A healthy response is, *"You are a wonderful boy, but it is not okay to hit your friend. You'll need to have a time-out and tell your friend you are sorry. Let's figure out ways to express your anger that don't involve hitting."*

A shaming response says, *"What a mean boy you are. Quit hitting your friend! No one is going to like you."*

We want our children to develop healthy guilt over their wrong actions. Healthy guilt says, *"I did something wrong."* Shame says, *"I'm a horrible person."*

Tips for Applying Logical Consequences to Promote Personal Responsibility

THE MOST EFFECTIVE way to teach children about right and wrong is to apply logical consequences to their behavior. This helps them learn how life and relationships work, how to control their impulsive behavior, and how to succeed at school, work, and relationships.

Our children need to struggle, persevere, and be tenacious. We need to let them fail so they can fight back and succeed. When they know they can rise up again after a loss or a disappointment, they can have hope for the future. They can have confidence that they have what it takes to meet future challenges, because they've persevered in the past. Our children also need to know that if plan A doesn't work, they can move to plan B.

The following tips are not designed to control your children to do what you want. They are meant to provide ways to gently teach your children in order to build life skills, strengthen their character, and help them persevere.

Make your Expectations and Consequences Specific and Clear

ENCOURAGE THEM FOR their progress and provide logical consequences to teach them when they do not follow through.

- "When you finish your homework, bring it to me to check and put it in your backpack. Then you can play with Jimmy."
- "You will need to put your clothes away and feed the cat before you can play with your toys. If they aren't done by 4:30, you can use $1 of your allowance to pay your brother to do your chores."

- "You may play video games for one hour. Set the timer. If you don't stop when the timer goes off, you will lose your turn to play tomorrow."

When our kids were six and eight, they started to make their lunches each night before school. They are human, so I knew there would be times they wouldn't make them or would forget to put them in their backpack the next morning. I sat them down and said,

"You are doing a wonderful job making your lunches. Because you're human, there will be times you may forget to either make your lunch or forget to bring it to school. I won't be bringing your lunch to you if that happens. There are two things you can do. You can skip lunch and eat extra when you get home, or you can use your social skills to mooch food off of your friends. When this happens, go up to them and say, 'I forgot my lunch. Does anyone have anything I can eat?'"

When They Make Poor Choices, Offer Empathy

OFFERING COMPASSION FOR the tough spot they find themselves in is so much more effective than lecturing them or rescuing them.

It's important to not say "I told you so" when your children tell you the mess they are in.

This just causes distance, and it trains your children to not open up or be vulnerable with you. It also removes you as someone who can help them learn from the mistake they've made.

Some possible responses include:

- *"I feel sad for you that you won't be able to go with us to the park today."*

- *"It must have been so hard to not do well on that test."*
- *"That's really too bad. I hope that works out for you."*
- *"That does sound like a tough situation. I'm curious to see how you'll handle this."*
- *"That does sound very frustrating."*
- *"I bet that is disappointing, since the other kids get to go."*

Combining empathy with keeping your consequence is a practical application of parenting with grace and truth. This balanced response helps your child know you understand, and it also shows that you will not change your consequence or react irrationally. On rare occasions, you may find out new information that may adjust the consequence.

Stay firm and empathetic. Do not react angrily. This helps your children face their own behavior, and the result of it. Otherwise they will focus on what a mean mother and father they have.

Here's an example that happened in our home. Our children did daily and weekly chores. I wrote these on a paper and put it on the refrigerator. Their daily chores had to be completed by dinner, and their weekly chores had to be done by 4:00 on Saturday.

We had a weekly tradition of going out to dinner every Saturday night at 5:00. The rule was if you didn't finish your chores, you couldn't go to dinner with the rest of the family. One time, one of our children didn't complete the chores and couldn't come. It only happened once.

I said, *"You didn't do your chores, so you can't come to dinner with us. You can go over to our neighbors and help her with some yard work. We'll bring you something back, and we look forward to you being able to come next week. I'm going to miss having you with us, and I love you very much."*

I set this up with our neighbor ahead of time, and it was very effective. For this to work, the child needs to do something unappealing at the neighbors. It won't work if they get to go over there and play video games.

Ask Good Questions

IT'S EASY TO lecture and have the right answers. This doesn't help your child become responsible. What does help is to ask thought-provoking questions. They help your children look at themselves and figure out how their actions are directly affecting their lives—for good or bad.

When they make a poor choice, wait a day or two, and then ask what they learned from what happened. We do this to help them learn from their mistakes, not to shame them for these mistakes. It's important to not tell them what they learned, or should have learned. If we do, it may stop them from learning from their mistakes.

Here's something I might say, *"It's so normal to make mistakes, I do it all the time. I usually try to figure out what I could have done differently. What did you learn from what happened?"* or *"Is there anything you would do differently next time?"* Even if they say no, it will get them thinking about this important question on their own.

Check chapter 12, "Coaching Your Kids through Life," for more great questions.

Coaching Yourself in Grace and Truth

BE YOUR OWN positive coach. I always joke that I have a coach on my shoulder helping me to do the right thing. *"Don't do that, don't say that, think of the big picture. Bite your lip and don't speak."* If I just respond without thinking it isn't pretty.

Adopt Compassionate Attitudes Toward Your Children

THE ATTITUDES WE have about helping kids learn about real life is incredibly important to how all this goes. Sometimes we get so surprised about the wacky things they do. *"I can't believe he did this! What was she thinking?"*

The reality is we shouldn't be surprised at all. It is important to remember that our goal is to teach and guide our children with consequences, rather than punishing them. The following statements will help you have a healthy attitude toward your children as they grow.

Grace and Truth Statements to Repeat to Ourselves:

- Children deserve politeness, respect, and caring.
- Children can learn to be capable and responsible, and they can handle their own problems.
- It is normal, natural, and expected for children to test the limits.
- It is normal, natural, and expected for children to fail as they are learning how to live in the real world.
- Kids will always do things that aren't good ideas—this is how they learn.
- We want kids to make as many mistakes as possible while still under our influence.

GRACE AND TRUTH STATEMENTS TO SAY TO OUR

- "It is normal that as you learn you will make lots of mistakes…this is how we all learn."
- "I'm sure you'll do the right thing, and if you don't, you'll learn something from the experience."
- "You are worthy of being treated with respect, and I expect you to treat me the same way."
- "You are capable of learning things on your own and making good decisions."
- "Life is not about doing things perfectly. It is about learning from most experiences and becoming a loving person, to yourself and others."
- "You can be kind to yourself when you make a mistake."

Remember to be flexible if you have a basically good kid who just made a mistake. However, a pattern of mistakes always needs to be handled seriously to avoid your child developing a character weakness.

GRACE AND TRUTH STATEMENTS TO SAY TO OURSELVES

- "It's normal for me to make mistakes as a parent. It's how I learn too."
- "I deserve respect, politeness, and caring. I can set boundaries with my child if I am being treated with disrespect."
- "I can be compassionate with myself when I goof up with my children."
- "I'm more than just a parent. It's good for me to take time for myself and recharge with ways that work for me."
- "It's okay to be continually learning as a parent."

Parenting our children with grace and truth is a reflection of the character of God. We can be balanced as we teach our children about boundaries and consequences, while applying compassion to our children and ourselves. Don't hesitate to ask friends for help and support. If your child is older and consequences have not been applied consistently, it will take some time to turn things around. Give yourself and your children time and compassion to develop new habits. It's not too late.

Now What? Where Do I Start?

1. Pray. Ask God for wisdom to help you know where you need to begin.
2. Ask yourself some important questions:
    - Which type of parenting style do I tend to operate: Permissive, Authoritarian, Dismissive, or Authoritative?
    - Do I have enough loving interactions (grace) with my children that would support implementing logical consequences (truth)?
    - Do I have enough truth to balance out my natural tendency to extend grace?
    - In a particular situation how can I show grace? How can I show truth?
3. Consider starting with one area:
    - Adding more loving interactions with my children.
    - Empathizing with the predicament my child is in.
    - Not rescuing my kids.
    - Letting my kids have more choices and input.
    - Setting consequences ahead of time and following through.
    - Asking good questions.

4. Come up with a plan for just one area, and work on that.
5. Speak to yourself with compassion. *"I like those compassionate statements in this chapter. I'm going to say them to myself a lot! It's normal for me to make mistakes as a parent. It's how I learn too. I deserve respect, politeness, and caring. I can set boundaries with my children if I am being treated with disrespect. I can be compassionate with myself when I goof up with my children. I'm more than just a parent. It's good for me to take time for myself and recharge with ways that work for me. It's okay to be continually learning as a parent."*

7

Helping Your Kids Cooperate

Be kind and compassionate to one another, forgiving each other, just as in Christ God forgave you.

Ephesians 4:32

HOW DO I get my kids to cooperate? Every parent wants the answer to this question. We have so much on our plates and often feel overwhelmed. We simply want them to cooperate!

KIDS WANT TO BE COOPERATIVE

YOU MAY THINK, *"Not my children!"* But it's true. They want you to be proud of them, to think they did a good job, and to see them as contributing and making a difference.

I saw the cutest example of this just the other day when I was getting gas. There was a mom, grandma, and ten-year-old boy in the car in front of me. While their car was filling up with gas, the mom was washing the windows with a squeegee. Her son really wanted to be helpful. She gave him a towel and then she'd squirt water, and he'd rub, she'd squirt and he'd rub some more. Honestly, he was probably just rubbing dirt around. She would say good job, and they were both laughing and enjoying one another. Pretty soon he wanted to wash the lights, so she'd squirt, and he'd rub. He was so proud of himself for helping her wash the car. His mom was encouraging his desire to help and cooperate. It was very sweet and a wonderful example of how kids really do want to cooperate.

Cooperation is a learned skill, not a genetic gift or character trait. If you're waiting for your child to start cooperating of his own free will—you might want to pack a lunch. This won't happen on its own. It takes consistent, effective skills to encourage your children to cooperate willingly on a regular basis. It takes practice, patience, and persistence on your part, but it is totally worth it.

Children are actually wired to cooperate, and when given the opportunity they're really pretty good at it. The problem usually arises when we make demands of our kids instead of requests. Believe me, I've done this more times than I'd like to admit!

At a very basic level we really do expect our kids to do what we ask, and to do it right away. That is such a lovely idea! We tend to make demands when we are exhausted and need them to do "this thing" because we're at the end of our rope. We're tired, and we need them to tie their shoes or pick up their toys right now! Rather than cooperating, they rebel against our intensity.

When they don't cooperate, we are disappointed and even surprised by their resistance. If we step back, we really shouldn't be. We are the same way. I know that my Heavenly Father would like me to do all sorts of things. I rebel and am sporadic about following the instructions God shares with me in His Word. He has compassion for me and loves me anyway.

We are just like our children. Our needs, the pressures of life, and human nature makes us vulnerable to bark out orders. When those orders aren't followed, the bark just gets louder. The following are ways to build cooperation and reduce power struggles.

WAYS TO BUILD COOPERATION

LISTEN

THIS MEANS REALLY listening to your children, even when they're not cooperating. Take the time to listen and figure out what is wrong. Often, they aren't cooperating because they are having a hard time or misunderstood what we asked.

When our daughter was two, she refused to eat her dinner. I made Hamburger Helper, and she would not eat it, which was unusual for her. She kept saying, *"No, no, no."*

I had her sit at the table for a while to see if she would try it. She wouldn't. It wasn't until she was four that she was able to explain what was going on inside. I mentioned the time she wouldn't eat and stayed in her chair for such a long time, and she said she wouldn't eat it because she thought the hamburger pieces were "dog poop" and she didn't want to eat them!

She didn't have the words to tell me at the time. What looked like defiance and a lack of cooperation was her taking a moral stand for her health! When your kids are taking a stand on something, it's a good idea to find out why. It's possible, of course, that they just don't want to do something. It is also possible they are having a genuine problem based on a misunderstanding of what is happening.

I wished I'd asked her, *"Honey, what do you think this is?"* or *"What will happen if you eat this?"* She might have been able to say, *"Poop,"* at age two if I'd asked a question. I just assumed she was rebelling, which was wrong.

They are always making associations that are incorrect. It's good to ask questions to make sure you understand what they are thinking. We often assume they have formulated thoughts inside about what they are doing or not doing. The reality is that they usually have no idea why they do things. When you ask questions, it helps them figure it out. Thought-provoking questions actually help them connect the left (thinking) and right (feeling) sides of their brain to work together and mature.

Be Consistent and Follow Through

I KNOW THAT'S easy to say and hard to do. We're not looking for perfection, just a "B" grade. Try to be consistent with the rules and not change them if possible. It is confusing to kids if one time they have to have to do their homework or chores before playing with friends, but another time they don't have to. If we are consistent with consequences, our children know we mean what we say and will be much more cooperative.

I remember how frustrated our kids were when we set a rule or consequence they couldn't wiggle out of it.

Once our son said, *"It's so hard having a mom who fallows through all the time."* I said, *"I bet it is. It must be awful when you make a great argument or try to get out of something, and I still stick to my guns. That has got to be frustrating."*

He hung his head and said, *"It is."*

Recently he was telling his new wife that when we said something, that was the way it was. He knew we meant what we said, so he'd better just do whatever it was.

Give Them Choices if at All Possible

THERE ARE MANY ways to offer choices. First, you only offer choices that you can live with and never offer choices that are not good for you.

There are times when children will not have a choice, such as needing to get ready in the morning. However, there may be a choice about the order they do things.

Giving them options helps reduce the tendency that we all have to rebel when we feel controlled or are given no choice. Giving them choices helps them think, and gives them the training they need to make good decisions.

Allow them to choose a **task to accomplish**, such as:

- *"Would you like to sweep the floor or dry the dishes?"*
- *"Would you like to empty the trash or unload the dishwasher?"*
- *"Would you like to wear your jeans, brown pants, or skirt?"*

You can let them decide **what order** they'd like to do things, such as:

- *"What would you like to do first, put on your pajamas or brush your teeth?"*
- *"Would you like to do your spelling or math homework first?"*

Another way to use choice is the **time-focused** choice:

- *"Would you like me to start reading your bedtime story at 8:00 or 8:05?"*
- *"Would you like to set your alarm for 7:00 or 7:10?"*

If a child **creates his own option**, simply say, *"That wasn't one of the choices"* and restate your original statement.

If a child **refuses to choose**, you choose for him. *"I guess I'm going to pick for you this time, maybe next time you can pick."*

It's important that when you give your children a choice that they learn to live with the consequences of their decision. It's also very important that you follow through.

So, if your little one is running amok in the grocery store, you can say,

"You have a choice. You can walk beside me or ride in the cart."

The minute he takes off, you can pick him up, put him in the cart, and say,

"I see you've decided to ride in the cart."

You want to consistently communicate that **they** are making the choice, rather than you making the choice.

"No, you could have walked beside me, but when you ran off, you made the choice to ride in the cart."

When they are learning, give them a chance to reconsider if they seem uncooperative at first:

"I know no was your first choice. I understand. How about if you think about it for a minute. Here are the choices: If yes, then ______; if no, then _________."

This gives them a second choice to be cooperative because they are learning.

Here's an example: you tell your child to pick up his toys and he says, *"no."*

You say, *"I know that 'no' was your first choice. I'd really like you to think about it for a minute because here are the two choices you have. One, you can pick up your toys and then watch your favorite show. Two, you can refuse to pick up your toys and help me wash the floor. I know at first you said no, but why don't you think about that and let me know in one minute. Whatever you decide is fine."*

Learning How to Make Good Decisions Takes Time

JUST LIKE LEARNING to ride a bike, it takes a lot of practice to learn how to be cooperative and make wise choices. No one learns anything right away; we learn a step at a time. Sometimes our kids need some extra help to be successful.

Offer to Lend a Helping Hand if the Task is Too Hard

WE OFTEN MISS that they get overwhelmed by big tasks or tasks that have too many steps…just like we do. Being asked to pick up all their toys might feel like us having to clean out our garage.

Let's say I get a burst of energy and decide I'm going to clean out my garage. This is no small task, since I haven't cleaned out my garage in years. I have good intentions, but when I walk into the garage it looks horrible. It is dusty with stuff stacked to the rafters. I take one look and walk back out. I feel overwhelmed, and I decide it is just too much to do.

Then I decide to calm myself down and consider that if break it into steps, I can do a little each day over the next week. I might also ask a friend to help.

This is what it is like for your children when they have to tackle a big task when they are little. You walk into their room, and say, *"You played with all these toys and need to put all of them away before you can watch your favorite show."* From an adult perspective, this request may not seem like a big deal, but to them it is as overwhelming as you walking into a garage that is packed with junk.

They may refuse, start to cry, or ignore you. What looks like a lack of cooperation may be a sign they are overwhelmed and have no idea where to start. It's important for us to understand this might be going on inside them. They don't have the words to say, *"This is completely overwhelming. There's no way I can do this. I don't know what to say, so I'm going to just cry, yell at you, or ignore you."*

You can help your child cooperate when you gently say, *"I know that is a lot to pick up. Let's do it together. Which would you like to pick up? Do you want to pick up the blocks, or do you want to pick up the train set?"*

Or, *"I know maybe folding a whole load of laundry is a lot to do. Do you want to fold the T-shirts, and I'll fold the socks?"*

Give Clear and Simple Directions

THEY NEED CLEAR instructions, appropriate for their age. This reduces confusion, increases cooperation, and gives them a chance to succeed.

- Don't make general comments that hint at what you would like done, such as, *"It would be nice if somebody helped me clean up."* Hinting doesn't work, and it won't get you the help you need. Plus, you don't want to teach your children to hint. Here's what works:
    - "I'm feeling overwhelmed and could use some help. Please unload the dishwasher."
    - "Please wipe off the counter so there are no crumbs, rinse the sponge, and put it on top of the dishwasher."
    - "Please put your dirty clothes in the laundry room by 5:00 p.m. if you'd like them washed."
    - "Please finish your math homework and bring it to me to check before you go to Susie's to play."

- Don't make it sound as if compliance is optional by starting your sentence with *"Will you? Could you? Would you?" or ending your sentence with, "Okay?"*
- Be very clear what is expected of your children. Make your request clear, short, and specific. *"Please put your dishes in the sink and wash the table," or "It's six o'clock. Put away your homework and come to the table."*

Younger children can only handle one or two instructions at a time. For older kids, be very specific about what you expect. For example, you may ask them to clean their room. You may have a very different idea than your child about what "clean" means. Be specific and ask them to make their bed, pick up their clothes, tidy their desk, pick up trash, and whatever else you'd like them to do.

It may even help to make them a list of what "clean your room" looks like and post in their room, in the bathroom, or on the refrigerator. Drawing pictures for nonreaders is also a good way to make your expectations clear. Ask your children to come and get you when they are finished, praise them for their hard work, and gently guide them if they need to do a little more work.

Use a Kind Tone of Voice

AS PARENTS, WE are exhausted as we juggle more tasks than are humanly possible! It is hard to interact with our children when we are worn out. If possible, try to use a kind tone of voice with them. It's easy to talk harshly when we are stressed out and have too much to do.

Fight against the feeling that your kids are disobeying you on purpose or that their lack of cooperation is personal. It isn't. They are learning hard lessons they don't want to learn. It's difficult for them to not always get to do what they want, have to do the hard thing before the fun thing, and obey even when they don't want to. It's normal to rebel against the hard parts of being a civilized person! It isn't a personal affront to you that they are having trouble adjusting to reality. Life is hard.

Give a Heads-Up for an Upcoming Task or Change in Plans

MAKE SURE YOUR children know in advance what is expected of them. For instance, if you are leaving a play date, give them some time to get used to the idea. Let them know you will be leaving in ten minutes and then remind them again in five minutes. They will be more likely to cooperate if they are prepared.

Part of what we are teaching is how to transition between events. This isn't something that comes naturally. Some kids and adults are better at it than others. It won't go well for kids or their parents when kids are given no warning when things are changing.

Being told *"We are leaving now"* or *"You need to do this right now"* will cause a child to be uncooperative because they are in the middle of something that's important to them. They haven't been given time to adjust. I wouldn't want to cooperate either if I was treated this way. They may rebel because of being spoken to harshly, rather than they don't want to do what is asked of them.

When our kids were little, they often didn't want to leave the park when it was time. I would tell them to hug or say goodbye to five things in the park they loved…like trees, the slide, the swings…and let them know we'd be back to see them soon. It really helped them transition from the park to the car.

Don't Compare Cooperativeness Between Children

THIS DOESN'T MOTIVATE them, even though we want it to. Saying, *"Jimmy is so good about putting his backpack away; try to be more like him,"* will not turn out well. We may think this will motivate them, but what it actually does is discourage them. Unfortunately, it can cause more sibling rivalry…and Lord knows we don't need any more of that! What does help motivate them is the next tip.

Praise Them When They Are Cooperative

I LOVE DOING this! Look out for when they are cooperating and lavish the praise. All of us are much more likely to do things that we get encouraged for.

Praise behavior that demonstrates cooperativeness more often than pointing out their lack of cooperation.

For example: *"I really appreciated how quickly you got ready, got your shoes on, got into your car seat, and buckled up when I told you we needed to get to our appointment."* You may even want to throw in a bonus such as: *"I think we can spend an extra ten minutes at the park today because you got ready so quickly."*

You want them to understand that when they're cooperative, good things happen. When you see your children helping someone, being kind to their sibling, or doing what you asked, make sure and point out how much you appreciate it.

Tell Them What a Difference They've Made to You

YOUR KIDS AREN'T able to figure this out on their own unless you connect the dots. They do not have much influence in their world, so it has a positive impact on them when they realize they made a big difference by being cooperative.

"Guess what? I have a little more energy to play a game because you helped fold the laundry."

"I feel happy that we get to spend extra time playing because you helped your sister with her homework."

"I was so glad to see you helping your teacher today at the end of class. I'll bet that really encouraged her. You are a very kind person."

EMPATHIZE WITH COMPASSION

DON'T BE SURPRISED when they don't want to do their chores. I don't want to do mine either. Let them know you get it.

"I know you don't want to take out the trash. I get it. This morning I didn't want to do the laundry, but I did because I knew you needed your baseball uniform for the game today. It really is hard to do chores when you don't want to. Go ahead and get that done and then you can go outside and play."

"Honey, I know you don't want to fold those clothes. I felt the same way about cooking dinner yesterday, but I wanted to make sure we had a yummy dinner, so I did it anyway. It's normal to not want to, but you will still need to do this chore before you can go out to play with your friends."

Your empathy really helps them because they feel known and understood, even if you don't change your mind about them doing their chores.

Empathizing with them doesn't mean they don't need to do what is expected. What it does is create an emotional connection with them. If you don't empathize with them, they will think you don't understand or care about how hard this is for them. Empathy reduces rebellion and increases emotional connection and cooperation.

Avoid Letting Your Emotions Take Control

TRY TO STAY calm when they aren't being cooperative. Don't yell, threaten, criticize, or belittle them when they aren't cooperative. Instead, state the problem, "There are dirty dishes and snack wrappers in the TV room."

Pause. Be silent. And stare at your children. It's amazing that kids will know exactly what you're thinking. Most often, they'll respond by cleaning up. If not, let them know the consequence if not picked up before dinner.

Give Them an Incentive if Needed

REMIND THEM THAT there are benefits to cooperating. Realize this is the beginning of them learning to be a good employee, be successful at school, and be a good friend.

For example:

"After you do your chores you can play video games for thirty minutes."

"Once you finish your homework you can play with your friends."

"After you eat half of your vegetables you can have dessert."

"Take the trash out before we go shoot hoops together."

Special Tips for Bedtime

MOST PARENTS HAVE issues at bedtime. There are some things we can do as parents to make bedtime less traumatic. Understanding why your kids fight bedtime and what you can do about it will help this stressful time go a bit easier.

Bedtime is a Challenge for Both You and Your Child

HAVE COMPASSION FOR yourself and your kids as you deal with this challenging part of your day.

They want to stay up; you want them to go to bed. We are all exhausted and not at our best. It is a precious time and a challenging time all at once. Kids open up at bedtime and talk about things that are bothering them. Parents want to listen and know what's going on in their hearts, but they are tired at the end of the day.

Talk to your kids about what it is like for them to go to bed at night. It will help them to talk about it, and it will help you understand why it is hard for them to go to sleep. Each child will struggle in different ways.

- *"What's it like for you when you know it's time to go to bed?"*
- *"What's the hard part?"*
- *"What's the nice part?"*

Besides getting to know them better, it will give you compassion for why they struggle. It will also help you come up with a plan to help your children with the parts that are hard about bedtime.

Common reasons include:

- Feeling scared. Children often feel afraid when it gets dark and they are alone. Developmentally, four and seven are common ages children are especially fearful, as their brains develop and they become more aware that there are bad people in the world.

- Feeling lonely. Sometimes it can be hard for little ones to be alone in their room, especially if they know their siblings and parents are still awake. Our daughter said it wasn't fair she had to go to bed alone. She pointed out that I didn't go to bed alone, I got to go to bed with Daddy. She had a point. Sometimes it really helps to understand their perspective.
- Not being sleepy.
- It's hard for them if they aren't sleepy. Listening to soft music or listening to a soothing audio book can help ease them into sleep.
- Believing their parents are "having fun" while they are in bed. Of course, we know this isn't true. Once I asked our son what he thought we were doing when he went to bed. He said we were up having fun—eating snacks and watching TV. No wonder he thought it wasn't fair! I explained that actually I was going to pay a few bills, do some laundry, and wash the dishes. I asked him if he wanted to trade places, so I could go to bed and he could do my chores? He said no and went to bed.

Parents Set the Bedtime, But Kids Can Have Input

IT'S HELPFUL TO give your children input into what happens just before turning off the light. You can give them the following choices:

- Light off, or a night light
- One drink of water before bed
- Read a bedtime story
- Prayers

- Cuddling time
- Trip to the bathroom

Come Up with a Written Plan and Post it in Their Bedroom

PLAN A NATURAL slow-down as bedtime approaches. Establish a rou-tine starting about sixty minutes before bedtime that deescalates the "fun." Turn off the excitement of the TV, stop computer games and screen time. Allow time to talk, read, and snuggle as part of the bedtime process. Take time to quietly chat during bath time, read a restful story, pray, sing them a song, and cuddle. This will give you time to connect emotionally with your children at the end of the day.

Talk to them about ways they can soothe themselves as they are going to sleep. Things like slow deep breathing, listening to soothing music, talking to God, and hugging their favorite toys can really help. Practice these ways with them.

Expect and prepare in advance for your children's usual two to three delay tactics. Get the issues handled before your child gets into bed. You might even encourage your child to handle the issues with you. *"I know it is hard to go to bed sometimes. It seems like it helps you get ready by going to the bathroom, reading a story, and getting a drink of water. Let's go ahead and take care of these steps."*

Then start with your own version of *"I'll be turning the lights out in ten minutes."* Use those ten minutes with your children to tell them how much you love them, are proud of them, and enjoy them. Enjoy talking, cuddling, or whatever you'd like, as long as it continues to help your children relax.

Give your children two reminders during this time to avoid an abrupt departure. Then say, *"I love you. See you in the morning. Good night."* If your children still require interaction, do not go into the room—talk to them from the door. If your children get out of bed, supportively (but firmly) instruct them to get back into bed and say a friendly (but firm) *"Good night."*

The good news is that there are lots of ways we can help our children cooperate. As we build a loving and compassionate relationship with our children, they will become more cooperative. Understanding and empathizing with your children as well as offering choices, using consistent discipline, and giving them lots of compassion will make parenting your children more enjoyable and less frustrating. You can do it!

Now What? Where Do I Start?

1. Pray. Ask God to show you what you might be doing to contribute to your children being uncooperative.

2. Which ways of building cooperation do I want to work on?

    - Listening more
    - Following through with logical consequences
    - Giving more choices
    - Speaking kindly
    - Praising them for what they are doing well

3. Think about which bedtime tips sound good and give them a try.

4. Speak to yourself with compassion. *"I get so frustrated when my kids won't do the simplest thing I ask! It is so hard, especially when I'm so tired all the time. It makes sense why I snap at them sometimes; being a mom is great*

but sure is a lot of work. It is good to know I'm not the only one who struggles with uncooperative kids. It's also good to know I can try a few things to help my kids cooperate more. I'm a good and imperfect parent, and that's okay."

8

Helping Your Kids Become Emotionally Healthy

Rejoice with those who rejoice;.
mourn with those who mourn.

Romans 12:15

WHY IS EMOTIONAL HEALTH SO IMPORTANT?

RESEARCH HAS SHOWN that even more than IQ, a child's emotional awareness (the ability to handle feelings and pick up social cues) will determine his/her success in all walks of life.[10]

Emotions drive our behavior, shape our values, and motivate us in the choices we make. We need our children to be fully functioning, happy, successful people.

As parents, it is tempting to focus on their misbehavior, not realizing they need help with the emotions that are driving their behavior. It would be like noticing a wall in my home is slightly off kilter and spending all my time making the wall thicker in certain spots so it looks straight. This will never work since it is the foundation holding up the wall that needs attention and care.

Emotional intelligence is the ability to recognize and understand emotions in ourselves and others. This basis for relating helps us manage and express our emotions and respond to the emotions of others in accurate and effective ways. Daniel Goleman[11] discovered that emotional intelligence is a skill that benefits your whole life, not just advancing in your career.

Another researcher named John Gottman did studies on both long-term marriages that work and children who are able to succeed at school and with their friendships. What he found was that the skills that help kids succeed at school and with friends are the same skills that help marriages succeed and thrive long-term.[12] So what we are learning in this chapter will not only help you with your children's lives and their future, but also with your relationships.

WHAT DID YOU LEARN ABOUT EMOTIONS GROWING UP?

MOST OF US, including myself, did not receive training on how to become emotionally healthy growing up. This is most likely because our parents were not taught about their emotions either. We were just thrown out there to deal with our emotions and do the best we could. How your emotions were handled growing up will greatly affect how you respond to your children's emotions now.

There are many opinions about emotions. Some see them as bad…something to be pushed away, ignored, hated, or controlled. Some see value in emotions but haven't been taught how to interact with them in healthy ways.

Others see emotions as helpful and enriching to life and would never want to live without the impact and guidance of their emotions.

Most advice to parents wrongly ignores the world of emotion. Most teaching focuses on how to get your children to not misbehave but disregards the feelings that are underneath, which fuel the misbehavior. This approach only results in short-term behavior changes while hurting the relationship between the parent and child. The more we ignore our emotions, the more power they have over us.

Emotions are good. God created emotions on purpose, to guide us, warn us, and bring us joy. He wants us to develop and mature all that He's given us—not just our minds and bodies, but our emotions and spirit as well. When we attend to our children's emotions, they get the message that, *"The inside of me is important too—not just what I do, how I obey, or what grades I get."*

Parenting with compassion involves learning how to deal with our own emotions in healthy ways, as well as our children's. We can learn how to be an emotionally healthy person, even if we were not taught how to manage emotions growing up. Let's learn together.

Characteristics of Emotionally Healthy People

- Able to regulate their own emotions and calm themselves when needed.
- Better at focused attention.
- Can relate to others and pick up important social cues.
- Have an easier time making and keeping friends.
- Better at work and school situations that require academic performance.
- Able to empathize and connect to other people.

When a child's emotions are noticed, allowed, valued, and paid attention to, they will be calmer inside and better able to relate, learn, and perform. The first ability to suffer in a child who is struggling emotionally is the ability to focus, shift, and sustain attention when needed.

If your children are trying to manage upsetting emotions, it will be hard for them to focus on math, science, or english, especially if they don't like these subjects. It's hard to study and remember what you're supposed to be doing when in turmoil inside.

Decide to Work with Your Emotions, Not Against Them

YOU MAY BE feeling a bit overwhelmed right now about helping your children with their emotions. It's very possible that you are not very comfortable with your own emotions. If so, you aren't alone. It's not too late to learn. I spent thirty years as a therapist helping parents learn how to understand their own emotions, so they in turn could help their children. As you work with your emotions, rather than against them, they will become less mysterious and overwhelming.

When you become more comfortable with your own emotions, you'll become more comfortable with your children's emotions. You'll be able to tolerate more of their feelings and do the probing necessary to help them understand and master their own emotions.

It's kind of like lifting weights. First you can lift twenty pounds, then thirty-five, then fifty. It's the same with your emotions. You can build up your emotional muscles when something difficult happens. You'll be able to say,

"Before I would've freaked out if this happened. Now I can keep myself calm, talk to other people for support, and come back and help my child process this difficult situation."

We all have reasons for why we feel what we do, kids and parents alike. I encourage you to talk to yourself with compassion:

"Whew, this is really hard. Breathe, hang in there. What am I feeling? What do I need?" and *"It's so hard to see him struggle. I wish I could make this awful situation go away. I want to pretend there's no problem...but there is. I think I need someone to talk to about how hard this is, and get some ideas about how to help him through this tough time."*

If you could use some help connecting to your own emotions in compassionate ways, please check out my book, *Give Yourself a Break: Turning Your Inner Critic into a Compassionate Friend.* I dedicate an entire chapter to "Being Compassionate with Your Emotions."[13]

See Your Children's Emotions as an Opportunity for Closeness and Teaching, Not as a Burden

THERE IS NO way to express how important this perspective is. Having this attitude toward our children's emotions and struggles changes how we view these challenging times. We have the most impact on our children when we treat them with compassion when they are insecure and raw.

As parents, we care about our children being equipped in all areas of their lives. You might say to yourself, *"I'm going to do what I can to help my children stay physically fit, and get whatever academic help they need. I also want to make sure that they learn to be emotionally healthy. I'm going to look for opportunities to help them process their emotions."*

When we look for these moments, they don't feel as overwhelming. This is in contrast to, *"I can't believe they did that, I can't believe that happened."* The reality is, why can't you believe it? It happens every week.

Instead, *"These outbursts are normal and are how she is learning to manage her emotions. I want to be able to be there for my children at these vulnerable times. It sure isn't easy though."* With this type of positive attitude, we can look forward to these moments as life changing opportunities to empathize, get closer to our kids, fill up their emotional tanks at vulnerable moments, and teach them ways to effectively handle their emotions. It is during moments like these, that we can convey that they are loveable and acceptable even in their painful moments.

Helping Our Children Become Emotionally Healthy

What Doesn't Work

WITHOUT MEANING TO, some of the ways we interact with our kids' emotions do not help them become emotionally healthy:

- Ignoring their feelings, or encouraging their emotions to go away quickly by distracting, ridiculing or minimizing them.

This is in contrast to valuing, empathizing, and understanding what is going on inside your child. When children's feelings aren't addressed, they are left to figure them out on their own…and that doesn't go well. They won't know what to do in the moment to deal with their emotions, so they just act them out in problematic ways. It also doesn't equip them to deal with their emotions in the future.

Our children come away with undesired effects of this style of handling emotions. They will conclude that their feelings are wrong, inappropriate, and not valid. This often generalizes to feeling a sense of shame inside—that there is something intrinsically wrong with them because of how they feel.

They may have difficulty regulating their emotions, and will not know how to allow and encourage emotional expression in others. Here's an example of how this may play out.

Eight-year-old Carolyn comes home very upset about how mean her teacher is. She expects her to have two math worksheets completed by tomorrow. She hates math! You know that her teacher is not mean, and can't believe that Carolyn is over reacting.

Your first thought is to tell her, *"This is not a big deal. Every student has to complete these, and you need to just get them finished."*

Your intentions may be good, trying to help her accept the reality of daily homework. Unfortunately, she may also get the unintended message that she doesn't know what she is talking about. She may start thinking, *"Okay, I thought I knew how I felt, I thought this was a problem, but I guess it's not. I'm stupid and don't know anything."*

A comment like this here and there by a parent won't give her this message. A pattern of dismissing her emotions over time will cause her to not trust herself. Our children need to trust themselves and their gut instincts. We want them to retain the ability to say, *"I can tell something's wrong here."* If they don't trust their instincts they will give their power away to other people later on. There are plenty of bad people out there who want to take their power, decide things for them and control them.

Let's say instead, that you take a deep breath, calm yourself down and decide to try to see it from her viewpoint. She's been waiting all day to come home. An hour before she leaves she finds out she has to do way too much math homework when she gets home. She's been fuming inside for an hour and can't wait to tell you all about it.

You know it is normal to come home with homework, and not a big deal. But from her point of view it is a huge deal. You decide to help her with her emotions and say, *"That is so hard. That was the last thing you wanted your teacher to say. You just wanted to come home and play and now you have to do math...which you hate. Let me give you a hug and tell me all about it."* You are amazed that over a few minutes she calms down. You helped her understand her feelings and comforted her.

After a few minutes you ask her, *"Well you will need to do your worksheets. What will help you do them? A snack, sitting at the counter while I work on dinner, or something else?"*

This gentle way of responding to her emotions helps her learn about her emotions, experience compassion for her struggle, and teaches her how to soothe herself when distressed.

- Focusing on outward behavior to the exclusion of the inner life of the children (their thoughts and feelings).

We don't help children with their emotions when most of our energy goes into limit setting and strict discipline. We may be so focused trying to teach them to do the "right" thing and accidentally criticize or reprimand their emotional expression.

Parents fall into these two unhelpful ways of dealing with their children's feelings because they often don't know what else to do. Unfortunately, when children's feelings are pushed away, both parent and child lose awareness of their emotions and focus on outward compliance. Children may become judgmental of themselves and others, and have difficulty relating emotionally.

What Does Work

THERE ARE MANY ways that we can help our children become emotionally healthy.

They need us to help them learn about the world of emotions. We want to let them know that God created our emotions to help us learn how we are doing on the inside.

One of the ways that helps our children, is our ability to tolerate strong emotions such as anger, sadness, and fear in ourselves and our children. If we are unable to tolerate our own emotions, we will not be able to welcome them in our children. If this is challenging for you, let me encourage you. You can learn to grow in this area.

Our children need us the most when they are struggling emotionally. The often missed beauty of these moments is the opportunity to teach your children about emotions, equip them with coping skills, as well as grow closer.

Responding Warmly to Them When in Distress

CHILDREN ARE VERY vulnerable when in distress. They need us to respond to them with compassion when they are struggling. It's easy to have a good relationship when everything's fine. Anyone can do that.

Children have no idea how to help themselves when distressed. They need us to help them go from intense feelings of anger and fear, to a state of calm, comfort, knowing that things will be okay again.

The first opportunity children have to learn how to calm themselves when they are babies. They come from the warm, safe environment of the womb where every need is met for them without uttering a word.

Suddenly they are thrust into the world via a rough ride, into bright lights, loud sounds, and someone smacking them on the bottom!

They experience intense needs that must be met by inexperienced parents who are trying to figure out what their cries and coos mean. When babies become emotionally distressed, they have no control over their emotions. They go "from zero to sixty" in a split second. They don't know what is wrong, just that things aren't okay. They need us to help them calm down, learn that comfort is available, and that they can become calm again.

We do this by picking them up and holding them close, while saying soothing words. Over time, they start calming down. This is the start of them learning to deal with their emotions. They learn that, *"I go from being really upset, then Mom or Dad picks me up, then I feel better and I'm okay again."* Of course, they don't have words at that age, but they have the sense that, *"I can go from being really upset to calming down."*

Babies continue to learn how to self-soothe when suck their thumb, use a pacifier or carry around a blanket. This is how they learn, *"I can soothe myself when I'm lonely or upset. When I go to daycare or am away from Mommy and Daddy for a while, I can bring my blanket and special toy, because I'm learning how to comfort myself."*

As parents, we can help them learn to comfort and soothe themselves when distressed, which provides them a healthy foundation for future relationships. The good news is that no matter one's age, it's not too late to learn these skills, even if we missed learning them growing up.

When our daughter was eight, her friend moved away and she didn't know what to do with her sad feelings. She cried about him moving away every night when she went to bed. Her grief wasn't resolving on its own, and I realized she didn't know what to do with these painful feelings.

I said, *"Would it help you to understand what's going to happen with your feelings over time?"*

And she said, *"Yes."*

I said, *"Well, for the first week you're going to feel really sad every night, and you may cry. Then next week, starting on Monday or Tuesday, instead of feeling this sad, you'll feel half as sad. And then sometimes at school every once in a while, you won't think about missing him. Then after a month, you'll think about him and be sad just one or two nights a week. Then in three months, you'll be really sorry he's gone, but you won't have that pain in your heart like you have now."*

Then she said, *"Oh, okay,"* and went to sleep. I realized she had all these emotions, and had no understanding that her painful feelings could lessen over time.

The next day she asked me, *""If I don't miss him as much, does that mean I don't care about him?"* I explained, *"When you notice not missing him as much, it doesn't mean you don't care about him. You will care about him forever and he will always be a favorite friend of yours. You'll always remember him, but it won't hurt as much."*

I was surprised how much this helped her. It gave her a context to understand her feelings and realize they would get less painful over time. This was her first experience of someone dear to her moving away, and she didn't know what to do with her painful feelings.

Increase Emotional Awareness…in Ourselves and Our Children

EMOTIONAL AWARENESS IS the ability to recognize what we are feeling, and what others around us are feeling. The good news is that we don't need to be perfect in our emotional awareness. It doesn't matter if when you label your child's emotions, you get it wrong. Here's an example:

Parent: "Is this really worrying you?"
Child: "No, it's not worrying me, it's irritating me."
Parent: "So it's really irritating you. What's irritating about this for you?"

It doesn't matter if we get it wrong, because it continues the conversation, and we find out how they are feeling. When we are emotionally aware, we know that emotions are present, valid, and need to be attended to. This is in sharp contrast to trying to make our children's emotions go away as fast as possible.

When our children were little, I really wanted to know how they were feeling, regardless of their behavior. I would often ask them,

- "Are you doing okay on the inside?"
- "Are there any hurt places inside that you haven't talked to me about?"

Sometimes there would be no problems to talk about, but other times I would get a list of ten things that they were upset about. It was a challenge at times, but that was fine, because I really wanted to know how they were doing, and talk to them about it.

- "I'm so sorry that happened, how are you doing?"
- "Are you okay now?"
- "What do you think would help?"

If you want to grow in your ability to be emotionally aware, you'll need time to notice what's going on inside. It can also be helpful to keep a record of your emotions. Sometimes we get so busy we don't pay attention to our emotions, until we are overwhelmed.

Give yourself time to be aware of your emotions. Try checking in with yourself in the middle of the day or at night and jot down a few notes.

- How am I doing today emotionally?
- What was a joy today?
- What was my biggest challenge?
- What emotions do I need to process, rather than letting them build up inside me?
- Who can I talk with about what I'm feeling?
- What would I like to talk to God about?

Help Them Label Their Emotions

AS WE'VE TALKED about before, our children need us to help them understand what they are feeling and what to do with their emotions. Their feelings often come quickly and intensely, and they often can't label them. Most children are able to pick their emotions from a list.

Here's a possible conversation:

Parent: "What you are going through is very hard. Are you feeling sad, anxious, confused, or something else?"
Child: "I'm sad. I'm not confused."
or
Child: "No, it's none of those."
Parent: [You ponder what else he could be feeling.] "Are you feeling hopeless, hurt, frustrated, or something else?"
Child: "Hurt."

Parent: "Oh, I'm so sorry that you were hurt by what happened. That does sound really hard. What hurt the most?"

As we help them label their emotions, we can then help them learn to have compassion for themselves and what they are going through.

Listen Empathetically and Validate Your Child's Feelings

SIMPLY PUT, RELATING to your children with empathy lets them know that you care what they are going through. You take the time to understand what they are thinking and feeling, and let them know that you understand what they are struggling with.

Growing up in a home without empathy is a very lonely, empty place. Without empathy, you feel you must always be happy, calm, and have a good attitude. There is no understanding or comfort for bad days, dumb mistakes, and the normal struggles of life.

In a home without empathy you learn to keep your mouth shut about what's really going on in the inside. You either withdraw into yourself, invest yourself outside the home, and/or come up with habits and activities that make an attempt to distract you from the painful and lonely places inside. TV, computer and video games, eating, drinking, drugs, pornography, and being glued to social media help in the moment, but they cause their own set of problems.

What you really need is a listening and caring ear, someone who can put themselves in your place, understanding the struggle, and offer help if needed.

Teach Them How to Regulate Their Emotions

KIDS NEED US to help them go from a state of distress to a state of calm. They simply don't know how to do this on their own. As we treat their distress with compassion, they will develop compassion for themselves.

Treating their distressing emotions with compassion helps them calm inside and gives them the ability to think through options and make wise choices. Anyone who is in emotional turmoil is likely to make poor choices.

It's better to address children's low level of frustration early on, rather than reacting to them harshly, when things are out of control. Intervening when emotions are at a lower level of frustration have a much higher rate of being resolved quickly with an ending that builds closeness and trust between parent and child.

I remember when our son was very upset about something. He was so upset that he was starting to hyperventilate a little bit, and he said, *"I'm just really, really anxious."*

I said, *"Lie down and start taking some slow deep breaths."* I explained, *"Your body is going into hyperdrive. Taking slow deep breaths will help your body slow down and help you be less anxious."* He said, *"Okay."*

It really helped him to know what was happening in his body and how to lessen his anxiety. We then talked about different ways to handle the problem he was dealing with.

Other ways to regulate emotions include taking slow deep breaths, listening to soothing music, being held, and praying.

For more tools for soothing yourself when distressed, please check out my book, *Give Yourself a Break: Turning Your Inner Critic into a Compassionate Friend.* I dedicate an entire chapter to practicing self-soothing techniques.[14]

Communicate That Their Emotions Are Good, While Setting Limits on Misbehavior

WE WANT TO give our children the balanced message that emotions are good and misbehavior is not allowed.

Here's a way to communicate this.

"Your emotions are good. They tell you that something is going on in the inside. That's normal. At the same time, you can't just express these emotions in ways that hurt you or another person. If you do, there will be consequences."

For example, your son hits his younger brother after he irritates him. After you talk with both of your children, you talk to the offending son.

"Honey, I know that your brother was irritating you. You being angry with him is very understandable. Sometimes I get irritated with your brother too. It's fine to have those feelings, but you can't hit him. Even though it's normal for you to be angry with him, there will be a consequence for hitting your brother.

"Here's what to do the next time your brother is irritating you. Come and tell me all about it. Let me know why you're upset and how you feel like smacking him. You will not get in trouble for coming to me with those feelings. If you hit him, you will."

When we value their emotions, they will learn to value themselves. This will then help them to take care of themselves in healthy ways.

Help Your Children Problem Solve the Difficult Situation

FOR CHILDREN TO benefit from our advice, they first need to feel understood. They have to know you hear them, understand what they're going through, and why they misbehaved. Once they do, they will be able to listen to what you have to say. If you respond right away with consequences or problem solving, they will feel misunderstood and won't be able to benefit from the wisdom you have to share.

> *Let no unwholesome word proceed from your mouth, but only such a word as is good for edification according to the need of the moment, that it may give grace to those who hear. Ephesians 4:29 (NASB)*

God wants us to respond to one another in the need of the moment, not with a predetermined, *"When she does this, I do this."* To know the need of the moment, we need to be aware of our children's emotions, empathize with them, and understand the problem. *What is my child feeling? What happened? What happened before she misbehaved? Does she need discipline?*

Remember, problem solving is only helpful after you listen, empathize, and understand their point of view. Going straight to problem solving never works. John Gottman recommends a structured way to solve problems in his excellent book, *Raising an Emotionally Intelligent Child.*[15]

The Five Steps of Problem Solving

1. If misbehavior has already occurred, set limits on this behavior.
2. Identify goals.
3. Think of possible solutions.
4. Evaluate proposed solutions based on your family's values.
5. Help your child choose a solution.

Here's an example of how I helped our son solve a big homework problem when he was in the fourth grade. He was sitting at the table getting ready to do his homework and was quite distressed. This was unusual for him. He didn't like doing homework, just like any other kid, but usually he could figure out what to do.

He was tearing up as he told me he had a huge project and he'd never be able to do it. He was very overwhelmed. I listened and empathized with how overwhelmed he felt. After he got it off his chest, I told him I'd like to help him figure out what to do. Would it be okay if I asked him a few questions? He said yes.

- *"When is the project due?"* One month.
- *"What do you have to do to complete the project?"* Read, flash cards, outline, map, and final report.
- *"How many pages of reading?"* 100.
- *"How many flash cards?"* 50.
- *"When is the outline due?"* Two weeks.
- *"When is the map due?"* At the end when he turned in the report.

As he started to tell me, he started getting upset all over again. This was the first major project he'd had to do over a month.

Before, his homework was either due the next day or in a week. Shifting to managing a month-long project was all new for him. His teacher had done a great job creating a handout that listed when each part of the project was due, but she hadn't taught her students how to break it up into small, manageable pieces.

I realized he needed help doing just this, so I decided to help. First I empathized again, *"I can see how this feels so overwhelm-*

ing, like there's no way you could do this. I think we can break it into small pieces that you can do a little bit on every day. I know you can do it."

A glimmer of hope appeared on his face. I proceeded to ask him more questions intended to help him break this huge project into pieces.

Mom: "Your project is due in a little over four weeks. There are seven days in a week. How many days a week do you want to work on it?"

Son: "Five, not on the weekend."

Mom: "So how many work days are there to work on it between now and when it's due?"

Son: "Twenty."

Mom: "How many pages a day would you need to read?"

Son: "Five."

Mom: "Could you do that?"

Son: "Yes."

Mom: "How many flash cards would you need to complete each day by the deadline?"

Son: "Three, I can do that."

Mom: "What's the best way to get the map and outline done in time?"

Son: "I'll work on them a little every day."

Mom: "Do you need any more help to figure this out?"

Son: "No. Thanks, Mom. I think I can do it."

I made sure and attended to his feelings first, and let him know I understood how overwhelming this was for him. He was then open to my help to solve his problem. If I had gone straight to problem solving, it wouldn't have worked.

Think about your own life. Imagine you have a friend or family member who's the problem solver or fix-it person. The reality is that those who are fix-it people have great ideas, because that is their strength. This isn't a bad thing, it's a timing thing.

Suppose you bring up a problem. You have a lot you want to say first. If Mr. Fix-It pops in with a solution too early, you won't be able to take it in, because you'll feel like *"You're not listening to me. You don't know what happened. You don't know what I'm talking about."* You won't listen to his solution, even if it is a great one.

We have much greater influence in our children's lives when we attend to their emotions and take the time to understand what has happened.

I love this quote by John Gottman.[16]

> *"Emotional Coaching does not mean an end to discipline. Indeed, when you and your children are emotionally close, you are even more invested in their lives and can therefore assert a stronger influence. You're in a position to be tough when toughness is called for. When you see your children making mistakes or slacking off, you call them on it. You're not afraid to tell them when they've disappointed you, when you know they can do better. And because you have an emotional bond with your children, your words matter. They care about what you think, and they don't want to displease you. In this way, Emotional Coaching may help you guide and motivate your kids."*

HELP YOUR CHILDREN GRIEVE

IT IS ESSENTIAL to both ourselves and our children to learn how to grieve through life's tragedies and disappointments. You may be surprised to find out that grief can be your best friend. It is God's answer to processing loss, pain, and disappointment. You may be afraid of these intense feelings and can't believe they are good. I know. But they are. God is an expert at grief and transitions, and He completely understands. He doesn't expect us to have our grief processed within a certain amount of time. He is faithful to love us and our children through difficult times.

Being able to grieve throughout my life has been a large part of getting through so many difficult times, including having a terminal illness. Grief helps us feel the emotions, adjust to reality, and eventually adjust to our new normal. When people do not grieve, they may remain stuck in what's happened to them, become bitter, anxious, or depressed, and withdraw from the good parts of life still available to them.

It is a true tragedy when the hardships of life not only take away what was lost, but future living as well. Learning to grieve through all losses, small or large, is what will help you and your children handle the realities of life and continue to grow and thrive. They will learn how to process grief by what you teach them, but even more by how you process grief.

Grief is full of ever-changing emotions like confusion, sadness, anger, loneliness, angst, anxiety, numbness, and vulnerability. Grief occurs in stages and is experienced uniquely by each person. The following are normal things to think and feel when grieving. I'm using personal examples of my grief process as I'm adjusting to having a terminal illness. Some of what I share will fit you, and some won't. Keep what is helpful and discard the rest.

Grief Stage One: Confusion

CONFUSION HAPPENS WHEN we have a lot of thoughts and feelings at one time. We're trying to sort out what's happened.

We may stare into space, forget things, not be able to stop crying, or feel like we can't think. We may also handle the initial confusion differently, setting our emotions aside to focus on the things we need to deal with right away.

I get confused a lot. The worst was right after I was informed that I had a terminal illness and there was nothing they could do. *How is that possible? No, I'm sure he didn't say that. I don't understand. What did you say?*

I go through another cycle of confusion each time my health worsens, and I lose the ability to do things I used to be able to do easily. As I grieve, I learn to adjust to what I can count on my body to do again for now.

COMPASSIONATE WORDS TO SAY TO YOURSELF…

"I've just been told devastating news. I can't believe it. I'm confused, mixed up, and overwhelmed. I don't have to figure out anything right now. I want to be a good friend to myself through this process. I'm not sure exactly how to do this. For now, I will take some deep breaths, then do something that is soothing for me and brings me a little comfort. I don't have to figure everything out right away."

GRIEF STAGE TWO: DENIAL

DENIAL HAPPENS WHEN we simply can't accept what has happened. When in denial we say things like, *What? This can't be happening. This isn't happening. There must be a mistake.*

It's normal to go into denial when hearing awful news. We fall into denial to get a break from our unwanted reality, it's just too much to handle. Being in denial is a normal part of grief, but it is destructive if we stay there. It is common to face what's happened and then fall back into denial. It's God's way of helping us adjust to loss gradually.

I was confused, discombobulated, grieving, and on overload when given my bad news. I still go in and out of denial from time to time. Being told I had a terminal illness was so difficult to take in. We live in a world where there are medical breakthroughs every day, right? There must be other options for treatment.

Compassionate Words to Say to Yourself…

IT WILL TAKE some time to accept that this has happened. Give yourself permission to take the time you need. For now, tell yourself:

"I've been given news that I'm not ready to accept. It's too much to process, too much to believe, and it hurts too much. I'm doing the best I can. I think I'll give myself permission to take the time I need to process all this, and surround myself with people who love me."

Grief Stage Three: Bargaining

ANOTHER PART OF the grief process is bargaining with God, ourselves, and whoever is giving us the bad news. It's like we don't like the deal we got, so maybe we can bargain for a different outcome by being a good person or persuading others, whom we hope have power, to give us better news.

When we find ourselves in the bargaining stage, we might say things like this:

I'll bet the doctor is wrong. Please, God, I'll go back to church and pray every day if you help me. I'll be a better wife/husband/parent/employee if you provide a miracle for me.

There is nothing wrong with trying to bargain for a different outcome. Bargaining is the step between denial and facing the truth. God is gracious to give us a way to ease into the reality of our situation. It's part of processing an unwanted reality.

I didn't do too much bargaining myself, but many people in my life did. They couldn't tolerate my prognosis being so dismal, so they "bargained" with reality by encouraging me to go on every natural, herbal, and nutritional supplement that existed, despite there being no studies to show their effectiveness. I tried many of these suggestions.

Compassionate Words to Say to Yourself…

YOU MIGHT FIND yourself in this bargaining stage for a while, or not. Try talking to yourself kindly like this:

"I think I'm still in shock. I'm trying to do everything I can to make what I've been told not true. It's normal for me to look at every possibility for a different outcome. I want to be kind and gentle with myself as I go through this process. It's okay for me to take the time I need to adjust."

Grief Stage Four: Anger

ANGER IS PART of the grief process. It is a natural response to getting horrible news of any kind. At some point after the receiving devastating news, it's normal to feel angry. *Why did this have to happen? What did I do to deserve this? I'm so angry about what has happened to my life and health. God, why did you let this happen?*

For some of us, anger comes easily. For others, not so much. Our anger can feel wrong, uncomfortable, and scary. As Christians, we may be afraid to acknowledge anger because it feels wrong to be angry with God or question the tragedies in our life. So we might bury our anger, which may make things worse, resulting in resentment, depression, anxiety, or additional physical problems. No one does this on purpose. How are you supposed to feel and process your anger if you've been told it is wrong, or have never been taught healthy ways to express it?

Our emotions are often layered, and often underneath anger is sadness, pain, fear, or shame. As we try to understand and learn from our anger, and express it in safe ways, it will often uncover deeper feelings of sadness and fear. The good news is that there are healthy ways to process our anger as we move through the stages of grief. Talking with a trusted friend or counselor, journaling, drawing, or expressing our anger out loud are all safe ways to process your anger.

Talk to God about all the questions you have as you try to make sense of what you are going through. You can do this in prayer, through journaling, or by talking out loud. Spend time in the Scriptures. Reading in the Psalms can be very helpful, as David expressed anger, disillusionment, and sorrow for the hardships he went through.

I felt angry when diagnosed with breast cancer. I felt even more angry when I was diagnosed with pulmonary fibrosis. That was such a low blow when the treatment for the first potentially fatal disease ended up giving me another fatal disease. My anger increased as I heard from four different doctors that they knew of this rare side effect, but none of them in a combined practice of eighty years ever had a patient who had this happen. Come on! My anger toward God, this disease, and life in general subsided as I allowed myself to have these angry feelings and talk to God and others about them. Anger still comes up from time to time with me, but now it's to a lesser degree.

Processing anger is not a one-time thing. It comes in cycles, just like the other emotions when grieving. When it pops up later, you haven't failed, there's just another layer to process. Be kind to yourself as you deal with your anger.

Compassionate Words to Say to Yourself…

"Sometimes it's hard for me to admit I'm angry about what's happened, but I am. It doesn't seem fair. I don't understand why God let this happen or isn't intervening. The truth is I am angry. It feels good to say it out loud…well, mostly. It's good to know I'm not in trouble for having these feelings. I think I'll be a good friend to myself by allowing myself to express these feelings in healthy ways that work for me."

Grief Stage Five: Sadness

SADNESS WILL FLOW in and out of you as you grieve. It is normal and healthy to allow yourself to feel sad regarding what's happened and how your future may be different because of it. I find myself cycling through the feelings of grief, and sometimes I experience times of peace and acceptance. Then something happens that sends me back into the sad feelings all over again. This often happens when my health worsens or when I'm reminded of a future experience I won't get to have, such as being a grandmother or enjoying retirement with my husband.

Waves of sadness flow through me. I allow myself to feel them. I process them through talking or writing, and they lessen over time. While these emotions are painful to feel, they are also cleansing to my soul, and they help me move forward. We have a companion in our sadness. One who knows. One who experienced in His time on Earth even more loss than we ever will. His name is Jesus.

> *Blessed be the God and Father of our Lord Jesus Christ, the Father of mercies and God of all comfort, who comforts us in all our affliction so that we will be able to comfort those who are in any affliction*

with the comfort with which we ourselves are comforted by God.

2 Corinthians 1:3–4 (NASB)

The LORD is close to the brokenhearted and saves those who are crushed in spirit.

Psalm 34:18

Blessed are those who mourn,
for they will be comforted.

Matthew 5:4

Jesus tells us that those who are courageous enough to grieve will be blessed and comforted. God draws near to us as we grieve. He is drawn to our vulnerability and suffering. He is here to comfort our broken hearts, soothe our fears, and give us hope. He is merciful to us during this grief process. He will bring us what we need to get through the grief, to get us to a better place emotionally. It is good to know that the Lord is close to the brokenhearted! He does not expect cheerfulness. God is compassionate and responsive. God is close—not far away.

Sometimes when overwhelmed with sadness, we may withdraw into ourselves and away from the people who love us. Even though it is hard, reach out for help and connection as you grieve. There are blessings in the relationships for you and for others. We aren't meant to go through sorrow alone.

Compassionate Words to Say to Yourself…

"It is so hard to go through these deep waves of sadness. Sometimes it feels like they will take me down. I want to be kind to myself about what I'm going through. It is such hard work to face reality and work through all these feelings. I

will let myself feel them for a while and then call a friend, or send someone a text to ask for support and prayer. There are many out there who love me, including God. They'll help me get through this."

GRIEF STAGE SIX: ACCEPTANCE

AS WE ACCEPT the reality fully, the pain lessens and we are able to make realistic adjustments to our new reality. Acceptance is not an end point, but something that happens slowly. As it ebbs and flows, we find more times of peace and meaning in this grief process.

I go in and out of acceptance much more now, still mixed with sorrow. I've shifted to looking for ways to have an impact on my family, friends, and others as my time wanes. I focus on being intentional with my time and energy, and I try to be sensitive to God's leading. My internal dialogue has changed. I'm able to accept this new reality most of the time, cherishing everyday blessings and soaking in the good that is here now.

We can return to the hope that God is bigger than all the losses of life. No matter how long our inventory of losses may be, we can find in God a peace and hope that reshapes our struggle.

COMPASSIONATE WORDS TO SAY TO YOURSELF…

"I'm not through all the stages of grief yet. I know that I will continually revisit them as I work through my grief. I'm not as afraid of my feelings as I was. I'm more at peace inside as I learn to be a good friend to myself during this very difficult time. As I allow myself to feel my emotions, I have more room inside to enjoy life and adjust to my new normal."

You can adopt what I shared above to help your children process the grief they feel when they go through losses, disappointments, and tragedies. They grieve over small things, like the top of their ice cream cone falling on the ground, moving, losing a friend, or going through major crises.

Processing grief in healthy ways while being compassionate with ourselves is the most powerful way I have found to get through the hardships of life. Please teach your children how to do this as well. It makes getting through the ups and downs of life so much easier.

It's not too late to learn more about your own emotional world and help your children learn about theirs. No matter what the age of your children, you can help them learn about the world of emotions.

Your children want to connect with you emotionally, even if they say they it's too late. Even if you weren't taught about your emotions growing up, you can learn. It doesn't matter where you start. The changes you make by relating to and building up your children's inner world will benefit your children for generations to come.

If your children are older and you are not used to relating to them in this way, it will take time, but it is not impossible. Hang in there, don't give up, and give it time. Treat your children like you would a good friend, with patience, compassion, understanding, and forgiveness.

NOW WHAT? WHERE DO I START?

Pray. Ask God for wisdom to help you figure out where to start. Pray for yourself and your children's development in this area. Ask God to give you wisdom and sensitivity to your own emotions as well as your children's.

1. Ask yourself some good questions:
   - What am I already doing well in this area?
   - Do I need to start more with working with my own emotions, or with my children's?
   - What is my gut-level opinion about emotions? Where did I get these?
   - Do I tend to focus more on ignoring my children's emotions, trying to get my children to stop misbehaving, or trying to understand and empathize with their internal world?
   - Do I know how to pay attention to my own emotions? Do I know how to soothe myself when I am distressed?
   - Which emotions in my children do I have the most trouble tolerating and empathizing with?
   - Am I expecting more emotional health from my children than I display myself?
2. When trying to empathize with your children's situation, try to imagine a similar adult-size situation. For example, anxiety about summer camp is comparable to the first day of a new job you're not so sure you are qualified for. Your children's traumatic moments are as valid as the ones we experience in our adult lives.
3. Practice listening to your children and try to figure out what the emotions are that go with their words. Check it out by asking, *"When you shared about what your teacher said in front of the class, were you more embarrassed, angry, or some of both?"*
4. Speak to yourself with compassion. *"It sure was hard this week to put everything down and really listen to my daughter. I really wanted to finish what I was doing and*

let her figure out her problem herself. I'm proud of my-self for sitting with her and listening to what she was struggling with. I know I didn't do everything perfectly, but I was amazed how much she calmed down after I put my arm around her, and she let it all out. We had a much better night after this. Good for me!"

9

Helping Kids with Anger and Fears

Fathers, do not provoke your children to anger by the way you treat them. Rather, bring them up with the discipline and instruction that comes from the Lord.

Ephesians 6:4 (NLT)

WE DUG INTO the world of emotions in the last chapter, and we learned a lot about how to help our children learn about their emotions and handle them in healthy ways. In this chapter, we'll cover the powerful emotions of anger and fear in more depth.

About Emotions

A CHILD'S SENSE of worth, value, and self-esteem are greatly affected by how their parents respond to their emotions. A child's emotions are more than just random feelings. They are a part of who they are, an essence of who they are. Along with a child's thoughts, their feelings are what makes them different from other people. When we reject, dismiss, and overlook a child's emotions...we are rejecting, dismissing, and overlooking them.

When a child's emotions are repeatedly downplayed, ignored, or put down, they will feel lowered self-esteem and shame…a pervasive feeling that they are of little value and worth. Damage occurs when a child's emotions are disciplined rather than their actions.

ANGER AND FEAR

IT IS NORMAL to struggle with these emotions, especially if you have been frightened by them in the past, or if the expression of these emotions were discouraged by someone in your life. But take heart. We, and they, can learn how to manage these powerful emotions.

Our emotions get triggered by our children's emotions. When this happens, we may shut down their emotions by denying, distracting, dismissing, or punishing the expression of these emotions. We don't mean to, it is an automatic reaction. It helps to understand how we get triggered by our children's expression of anger and fear.

Some good questions to ask ourselves are:

- "What gets brought up inside of me when my children are angry or fearful?"
- "What does my children's anger or fear remind me of? What do I need?"
- "What memory or feelings are triggered inside of me when I have a strong reaction to my children's emotions?"

It can be very upsetting when we respond to our children's emotions in ways we don't want. This happens when past unresolved pain get triggered inside of us. It happens to every parent. You aren't alone in your response. Later in the chapter I share things you can do to work through your own unresolved anger and fear to improve your life, and better respond to your loved ones.

For parents to be effective in helping their children with anger and fear, they need to understand these emotions, and what they are trying to tell us. It helps to put ourselves in our children's shoes to understand what they are feeling and why. We use empathy to help us understand what our children are going when they are angry or fearful, by asking ourselves,

- "What might be happening inside of my child?"
- "What is going on underneath all that anger and fear?"
- "What would it be like to be three and be having a great time playing, and then be told abruptly to put down your toys and get in the car and go somewhere you don't want to go?"

You'd be pretty angry.

- "What would it be like to be little, and not have the ability to think through things logically, and be really afraid of something?"
- "What would it be like to have your mom and dad be mad at you for being afraid, and not be able to know logically that there really aren't monsters in your closet?"

This would leave a little guy feeling alone and in trouble without tools or help to handle his fears.

Essential Attitudes for Helping Children with Their Emotions:

In *Raising an Emotionally Intelligent Child*, John Gottman talks about parents like you who courageously seek to join their children's emotional world,

"I call the parents who get involved with their children's feelings 'Emotions Coaches.' Much like athletic coaches, they teach their children strategies to deal with life's ups and downs. They don't object to their children's displays of anger, sadness, or fear. Nor do they ignore them. Instead, they accept negative emotions as a fact of life and they use emotional moments as opportunities for teaching their kids important life lessons and building closer relationships with them."[17]

What a wonderful way for us to view our emotions as well as those of our children. In order to develop compassion for their emotional struggles we need to look at emotions differently:

- Feelings are normal. As a parent, I want to help my children grow and mature in his/her ability to tolerate and appropriately express their emotions.
- Kids are all emotion when little, and very little thinking occurs, if at all. Over time, we want to help them learn to think through situations, rather than only acting out of their emotions.
- God made anger and fear to help us learn about ourselves and what we need. We want to validate our children's emotions, while at the same time, teach them how to express their emotions in ways that don't hurt themselves or another person.
- Before age six, kids have very little ability to think through and analyze their behavior. They can learn that if they do A, then B happens, but they are unable to think through how their behavior affects or hurts others. Some-

times we expect them to be farther along than they are able. Don't worry they will learn over time.

HELPING YOUR CHILDREN WITH ANGER

EVERY PARENT HAS seen their children hit, push, yell, and misbehave when angry. As parents, it is important to remain balanced in our response to our children when they are angry. We want to figure out whether these angry responses are normal or not.

In other words, is this behavior what every child goes through as they are figuring out how to manage their anger, or is this the beginning of a long-term pattern?

DISTINGUISH BETWEEN ANGER, ASSERTIVENESS, AND AGGRESSION

IT IS IMPORTANT to know the difference between anger, assertiveness, and aggression. This will help us know how to help our children express their anger in healthy ways.

Anger – Anger is a God-given feeling that results from being hurt, or the fear that you will be hurt. It is anger's motives, forms of expression, and effects that determine whether it is sinful or appropriate. Anger is a feeling, rage is a behavior. Anger is experienced on a continuum (mild to severe):

irritation upset frustration mad resentment aggression hostility hatred violence rage

Assertiveness – Standing up for yourself in an honest and reasonable way that doesn't hurt the other person. Assertiveness respects both your own needs, as well as the needs of others.

Aggression – Standing up for one's self in hurtful and inappropriate ways that violates the rights and welfare of another person. The heart of aggression is hurting another person.

Children who sometimes use aggressive behaviors either have not learned how to use positive skills to solve problems, or forgets to use the skills they know.

Ask yourself these questions about your children's behavior:

- Are the negative behaviors occurring in a situation most kids would have trouble with such as sharing, or does my child resort to anger every time he/she wants something or has to solve a problem?
- How often are aggressive behaviors occurring?
- How severe are the behaviors?
- What happens when your child does not get his/her own way? Do the behaviors worsen?
- Are your children's negative behaviors worsening (becoming more violent and hurtful)?
- Are others afraid of your child?

What Does the Bible Say about Anger?

God explains in Scripture that there is a way to be angry without sin.

> *"In your anger do not sin": Do not let the sun go down while you are still angry, and do not give the devil a foothold.*
>
> Ephesians 4:26–27

Anger in and of itself is not wrong. Righteous indignation is directed against those who act against God's standards of fairness, justice, and goodness. The anger expressed focuses on the wrong done. We get into trouble when the unresolved anger results in destructive and inappropriate actions that hurts others and yourself. Examples of destructive expressions of anger include: lashing back; yelling; and physical, emotional, and sexual abuse, which shames the character of the other person.

There is a form of "righteous anger" that in its purity only God really can express. Christ's expression of anger in overturning the tables in the temple was an expression of righteous anger as He said, *"Zeal for Thy house will consume me"* (John 2:14–17). For additional Biblical help with anger, see *Praying God's Word* by Beth Moore.

God cautions us about being quick to anger:

A hot-tempered person stirs up conflict, but the one who is patient calms a quarrel.

Proverbs 15:18

Do not associate with a man given to anger; or go with a hot-tempered man.

Proverbs 22:24 (NASB)

As with all emotions, we ultimately need to bring before God the underlying issues that are driving the anger. Anger is a secondary emotion. What this means is that there are always other feelings under the anger. The most common feelings that are felt a split-second before the anger is felt are guilt, inferiority, fear, trauma, pain, and hurt. This is very important to know because healthy and effective handling of anger must address these underlying emotions.

It is important to remember that a child who is very angry is a child who is in a lot of pain. The more anger and rage a child displays, the more pain and hurt he/she carries. What our child needs is our compassion and help, not our wrath.

Appropriate Ways of Handling Anger Must be Learned

NO ONE INSTINCTIVELY knows how to handle anger in healthy ways. These skills must be learned. Most of us misunderstand anger—why we feel it, how we express it, and how we can change the way we deal with it. Part of our job as parents is to help our children learn to manage their anger, so they have skills by the time they leave home. We want to begin anger training when very young, but we shouldn't expect to see our children exhibit some of these skills until six or seven.

Be encouraged that anger has a positive side, when it is controlled and used to effect positive change. There are situations in which we should feel righteous anger—when we see behavior and attitudes that harm innocent people or defame God. Even then, our anger is to be controlled and expressed appropriately.

Responding to Your Children's Anger

WHEN YOUR CHILDREN share their emotions with you, be very careful in how you respond to them. It is a gift of their real self. They are telling you, *"I'm going to share a vulnerable part of myself with you. I'm going to be real with you. Will you accept me? Will you shame me for the feelings I'm sharing with you?"*

If your children's feelings are shamed, they will shut down and stop sharing their real feelings on the inside. They will instead share the "acceptable" parts of themselves, but you will have missed access to the real child on the inside. Children can only suppress the emotional pain they carry for so long, and over time these emotions will be expressed, harming others as well as your children.

Strong anger takes away our ability to reason. It is normal to be angry with our children. We need to be very careful with how we express that anger to them. Anger directed at young children is terrifying, especially when it comes from a parent. A child is defenseless against a parent's anger, especially when young. Their greatest fear children have is that their parents will be angry with them and not love them anymore.

When appropriately expressed, working through anger can bring parent and child close as they work through difficult situations. When parents are able to tolerate their children's anger, children will feel known and accepted as areas of hurt and anger are shared and treated with compassion.

All parents occasionally lose it with their children, for understandable reasons. We are stressed, have so much to handle, and let's face it, our kids can be infuriating at times! Even when we blow it, we can go to our children and apologize. We can listen to their feelings and reestablish trust.

There are many reasons we may have trouble handling our anger in healthy ways. In order to help our children with their anger, we need to understand our own reactions. People vary widely on how comfortable they are with anger.

- Anger may have been an acceptable and appropriately expressed emotion, allowing you freedom to express it in healthy ways.
- You may have been harmed in the past when others lashed out at you in anger. As a result, you may become fearful when anger is expressed.
- Someone else's anger may have caused emotional or physical injuries to you or others, which may cause you to be fearful of your own expressions of anger.

- You may have been taught that anger is an "unspiritual" emotion and should therefore be resisted or denied.

TWO UNHEALTHY WAYS OF EXPRESSING ANGER

OUR GOAL IS to help our children express anger in healthy ways. Of course, they will make all kinds of mistakes and express their anger inappropriately as they are learning. We want our children to express their hurt and anger to us. If we do not, they will express their anger in unhealthy ways:

1. *Overtly* – Verbal and physical expression of anger, such as yelling, screaming, hitting, dirty looks, and shaming comments.
2. *Passive-Aggressively* – Anger expressed through actions, rather than words, such as: withdrawal of love and affection; saying yes but not following through; gossip; sarcasm; being late; and not keeping promises. Suppressed anger may also come out in physical symptoms such as headaches, sadness, depression, anxiety, and other physical problems.

Other possible signs of passive-aggressive anger in kids: grades falling, shoplifting, broken promises, being late, sneaking out, withdrawal, promiscuity, drug use, or not doing chores or homework.

Not all of these symptoms indicate a child who has suppressed anger. A wise parent will consider the possibility that underneath these behaviors may be some stored emotional hurt and anger that your child doesn't know how to express in a healthy way. Although it is difficult, approaching your children with compassion really helps as you seek to understand their underlying pain and misbehavior.

Practical Tips for Dealing with Your Children's Anger

Work with Yourself

- "Everyone should be quick to listen, slow to speak, and slow to become angry, for man's anger does not bring about the righteous life God desires" (James 1:19–20).
- Be aware of your feelings…don't ignore the subtle signs of anger.
- Be honest if you realize you have a problem with the way you express your anger. Exploding and unloading your anger on your children or spouse is damaging and will increase your children's rage and misbehavior.
- Don't pretend that the effects of your anger are no big deal. Be willing to see that both the overexpression of anger and passive expression of anger are destructive to your relationships.
- When you notice you are angry, work on slowing your system down by taking slow deep breaths, taking a walk, listening to soothing music, saying calming things to yourself, and praying for God to help calm you and see things in perspective.
- If you are unable to make much progress on your own to work through recurrent anger, get help through a book (see bibliography), a support or accountability group, or counseling.
- Ask yourself some important questions:
    - How was anger expressed in my family of origin?

  - What are my beliefs about anger?
  - How do I tend to express my anger?
  - What degree of anger do I typically feel?
  - What emotions often underlie my anger? What are the roots of these emotions?
  - Are there any ways to directly deal with these emotions, rather than act them out through anger?
- Remind yourself that you want your children to verbalize their anger, otherwise it will come out in their behavior. We don't get the choice that they won't get angry. We want to teach them to express their anger in healthy ways.
- Because children are young and immature, their verbal expression of anger will almost always come across to the parent as disrespectful, inappropriate, and childish! It's actually okay that their expressions are childish. It's when our expressions of anger are childish that we have problems!
- Remind yourself that it's normal for kids to get angry. Develop some encouraging self-talk to keep you on track when your child is expressing anger toward you. *"It's good she is verbalizing her anger. This means that she is learning how to recognize her feelings and manage her anger."*
- Remember it's a process. Encourage yourself that your child is better at expressing anger than he was a year ago. Tell yourself, *"I'm helping him develop a skill that will benefit him for the rest of his life."*
- Remember to breathe, slow down, count to ten, and not be reactive. Tell yourself, *"I'm giving my child a huge gift by letting him express his anger verbally. I'm helping him not become passive-aggressive or act it out in his behavior (as much)."*

Work with Your Children

- When your children are angry, really listen to what they are saying. Put yourself in their shoes and validate the feelings they are sharing. When we unknowingly refuse to do this, we make it worse. They try harder to get us to understand how upset they are by escalating their behavior. You can validate their feelings without endorsing their behavior.
- Gently talk to them about what they are feeling.
    - "Tell me about what's bothering you. I'm all ears."
    - "You seem like you are having a hard time. I'd like to know how you are doing."
    - "Yes, I can see you are very angry right now."
    - "You wish this was different. You wish I'd change my mind. It's hard for you that I won't. I can see why you're feeling angry."
    - "Is there more?"
- Your children may need you to help them identify their feelings, especially the ones that are under the anger. When we do this, their anger decreases.
- Set limits on their behavior, not their emotions. "Yes, I know you are upset and angry, and you have reason to be. However, you cannot throw your dinner on the floor or hit your brother. There will be a consequence for what you did, but I'm very sorry for the hard time you are having right now."
- Take a look at what your child has shared. Does he/she have a point you need to consider? Do you need to apologize for something? Is there new information to consider?
- If your child is really out of control, help him slow down his emotions and behavior so he can address the underly-

ing feelings that occurred before the anger was expressed. The point is not to get rid of the feeling, but to reduce the intensity of the feeling so he can talk about it.

- Teach your children to take a break when very angry in order to express all that energy. They can do something physical (take a walk, jump on a trampoline, ride a bike, or take a run) or relaxation focused (breathe deeply, pray, or take a shower). The goal is to help your children calm down enough to identify their feelings and express them verbally.
- When children express anger in unhealthy ways, they need to make amends for their behavior and ask forgiveness. Apologies are nice, but making amends makes the effect of their anger more real. It helps them realize the effect their anger has on others, as well as the cost to themselves. Examples include doing chores for the person they hurt, or paying for the item they destroyed. This is a skill that takes time to learn. Try to praise your children for any progress, no matter how small.

Helping Your Children with Their Fears

> *"Fears are survival mechanisms. They're the ordinary responses to unusual, and therefore, potentially dangerous stimuli. When they're normal they serve us well. When they get out of hand they can damage or destroy us. They can be crippling and self-fulfilling, and that is so unnecessary it's tragic."*[18]

- Fearful feelings are a part of life. We love our children deeply and don't want them to live with fear. We can really benefit from God's wisdom by looking at how He interacts with us during fearful times. The Bible offers us courage and hope during our fearful, sad, and discouraging times. There are many, many verses in the Bible that tell us that God is with us when we are afraid and in our darkest moments.

- We can walk through tough times because God walks with us through the valleys. God's example is not to ignore fearful times, but instead He comforts us with the knowledge that we are not alone…even in the toughest of times.

Fear not, for I am with you; Be not dismayed, for I am your God. I will strengthen you, Yes, I will help you, I will uphold you with My righteous right hand.

Isaiah 41:10 (NKJV)

When you pass through the waters, I will be with you; And through the rivers, they shall not overflow you. When you walk through the fire, you shall not be burned, nor shall the flame scorch you.

Isaiah 43:2 (NKJV)

Yea, though I walk through the valley of the shadow of death, I will fear no evil; For you are with me; Your rod and Your staff, they comfort me.

Psalm 23:4 (NKJV)

The LORD is near to those who have a broken heart, and saves such as have a contrite spirit. Many are the afflictions of the righteous, but the LORD delivers him out of them all.

Psalm 34:18–19 (NKJV)

- Notice how our comfort comes from knowing we aren't alone during our difficult and fearful times. God understands how hard life can be. He wants us to know, *"Life is hard, but I will be with you. Just reach out to me, and I'll be there."* He's our model for how to help our children through difficult times. Our children need us to be with them in their fearful moments and help them develop coping mechanisms.

Facts about Fears

IF YOU FEEL clueless about what to do with your children's fears, join the club. Knowing how to respond to children's fears is hard for lots of good reasons. Small children rarely ever understand their fears, so they find it hard to put them into words. We probably weren't given much help to understand and manage our fears growing up either. Sometimes it can feel like the blind leading the blind. I'm here to help.

Kids have different fears at different ages. By helping your children work through their fears, it equips them for the next stage of development and helps contribute to a solid sense of themselves in the future.

Unresolved fears steal many of life's joys from adults and children alike. It's hard to be creative, carefree, and ready to take on the world, if you are having to manage fears on the inside.

Fears have value: they let us know to watch out for something new or scary. They help us mature and grow psychologically. As children get older, they turn us to God, creating dependency on Him for all we can't control. Without fears children cannot grow emotionally; just like without exercise, our muscles cannot grow.

Fears do not come from a place of logic, and they never, ever respond to logic. Even if you feel like it, bite your lip when you are tempted to explain that there is no such thing as a ghost, or there is no monster under the bed.

Please don't shame your children for their fears, such as calling them a baby, and insisting they be a "big girl" or a "big boy." This gives them the message that they shouldn't be afraid and that there is something wrong with them.

The truth is they are having a normal fear, and there is nothing wrong with them.

What Helps

Come Alongside Your Child

> *"A journeymate is a person who understands a child's fears and problems and walks beside the child as the child resolves them, guiding if needed. The journeymate, therefore, must be older, wiser, and more mature than the child. The journeymate does not resolve the problem for the child. The child must do that. A journeymate cannot spare the child grief or struggle, but he or she can share it."*[19]

We are the ones casting a little bit of light on the scary places. We come alongside our children as they learn how to deal with and master their fears. Our presence makes sure they don't have to tackle their fears alone. When children handle their fears on their own, they come up with childlike solutions that don't work, and the fears often plague them for a lifetime.

Examples of this are eating, drinking, or drugs to soothe their fears; withdrawal from others; obsessive habits; perfectionism; and overuse of the internet.

Address the Fear from Your Children's Perspective, Not Yours

IT'S NORMAL TO think about your children's fears from an adult perspective, because we're adults! While understandable, it doesn't help them very much. What does help is taking the time to see the fear from their perspective. *What is it like to be three and going to preschool for the first time? What is it like to be five and have a huge black dog bark at you from behind a fence? What is it like to be ten and having to give your first oral report?*

We know these challenges generally work out okay, but our children don't. They are scared and intimidated and have good reason to be.

Empathize with Your Children's Fears

WE'VE BEEN LEARNING about the power of validation and empathy in prior chapters. Nowhere is it needed more than to help your children deal with their fears. In the above examples, allow your child to be afraid, empathize, and ask questions.

The child who is scared of preschool:

> Parent: How do you feel about going to preschool?
> Child: [Clings to your leg.]
> Parent: It looks like you're a little scared to go.
> Child: [Nods.]
> Parent: That makes sense. This is your first day and you don't know what to expect. I felt scared when I went to preschool for the first time. It's normal to feel scared when you do something new. Let's go together, and I'll help you figure out what to do.

The child scared of the big barking dog:

Big Black Dog: [Barking loudly from behind the fence.]
Child: [Crying and hanging onto you.]
Parent: [Picks child up, or bends down to hold him or her.] I know you're scared. That scared me too. Let me hold you for a while. You're okay. I'm so sorry that happened.
Child: I thought he might bite me. [Crying.]
Parent: I bet you did, no wonder you were scared. I'm glad he's behind the fence and can't get to us. I know that was scary. Let's go somewhere else. Let's both tell ourselves, "I'm going to be okay."

The child nervous about giving her first report:

Child: I don't want to go to school tomorrow.
Parent: Really? How come?
Child: I just don't want to go.
Parent: Is something happening? Is it this the day you give your report?
Child: Yes, I'm scared. I'm afraid I'll goof up and all the kids will laugh at me.
Parent: That makes sense. I remember how hard it was for me to give my first report. I was shaking and didn't think I could do it.
Child: You were? You talk in front of people all the time.
Parent: I don't get nervous now, but I sure did the first few times. It's normal to be nervous.
Child: Thanks, Mom. I thought I was the only one who felt this way.
Parent: Is there anything I can do to help? You can practice on me, and I'll be very encouraging!

Child: No, it just really helped to talk about it and realize it's normal to be scared.

After Listening and Empathizing, Share Some Facts That May Help

Regarding the above examples:

The child who is scared of preschool:

"You may not know this, but there are other kids who will be scared too. They need a friend like you. The teachers know that kids will be scared on their first day, and they have special snacks and toys to help make the first day easier."

The child scared of the big barking dog:

"I know it's hard to believe, but he was barking because he was scared of us. He didn't know if we were going to try to hurt him. We would never do that, but he didn't know it. Let's go somewhere else, and we won't have to hear him bark anymore."

The child nervous about giving her first report:

Parent: Do you think other kids will be scared too?
Child: Probably.
Parent: What do you think would help them?
Child: Tell themselves to take a big breath, and it will be over soon. Other kids are scared too.
Parent: That sounds like good advice. Do you think you could tell yourself that too?

THE BASIC FEARS BY AGE

THE BABY STAGE: NEWBORN TO TWENTY-FOUR MONTHS

THE FIRST FEAR we all deal with is being abandoned. Deep down, children know that they depend on others for everything such as love, affection, food, drink, shelter, clothes, protection, and "being with me." Children would die without others. There is not one need children can meet themselves.

Children's ability to trust forms at this age. *"Will someone come when I cry? Will I be taken care of? Will I be protected from bad people?"* If children are cared for without being neglected, abused, or left too much, they will form the ability to trust and make solid emotional attachments. Problems show up in older children and adults if this need has not been adequately met. The effect of poor emotional attachment shows up as inconsistency in relationships, inability to make solid emotional attachments, and emotional distancing in relationships.

The major task of this age is object constancy, knowing that when mommy or daddy leaves, she or he will return. What can get in the way of achieving this task arise in two basic ways:

1. Not leaving children much at all. They need to have you leave and tolerate the fear of being left for a short period, then return. Children learn their parent does come back.
2. Leaving children more than they can tolerate, so that deep fears begin to grow inside. When you do have to leave, always say, "*I will be back.*" That seems so obvious to us, but not necessarily to children, especially at first.

When you are away, provide items to comfort them: teddy bear, blanket, pacifier, or picture of the two of you together. Other ideas include letting them wear one of your shirts, making a recording or video of you singing to them, talking to them, or reading them a story.

If you are in a situation where you need to leave your children for longer periods of time, try to make sure the person caring for your children is as consistent as possible. If possible, have your children cared for in your home, or with just a few other children. Sometimes this is not possible, so in those cases, try to provide as much comfort for your children as possible.

Your children need to go through these periods of separation. They learn you'll come back. Over time, they will be able to feel your presence and trust you even when you aren't there.

The Preschool Stage: Three to Five Years

IN EARLY STAGE of preschool (age three), the second fear is felt: *"Can I lose Mommy and Daddy's approval?"* By age four or so, children's fear shifts from losing their parents to *"Will I lose their approval if I mess up? Oh, and by the way, how will I know if I'm messing up?"*

We want to teach children about right and wrong through consistent gentle discipline beginning around eighteen months. As children experience consequences from wrong behavior they learn:

- If I do the wrong thing, bad stuff happens.
- Even when I do wrong things and they don't like it, they still love me.

Between the ages of three and four, children's conscience develops from nothing to something. They begin the growth of doing the right thing in part because their conscience says it's wrong.

Before this, they only do the right thing because they know they'll get disciplined. When kids aren't disciplined consistently they will misbehave just to try to figure out where the line is. They will also begin to develop entitlement, which means "rules are for others, not for me."

Another way children's fears appear is when they transfer their fears onto objects. It's less scary than feeling them head-on. At this stage, kids tend to be afraid of various types of things: loud noises, sleeping alone, seaweed, large objects, and weather.

- Unhelpful response: "Oh, that big box won't hurt you. You have nothing to be afraid of."
- Helpful response: *"It's okay, Daddy is with you. It's okay to be afraid of that. I'm here to protect you."* This can be said in words or by picking up your child and comforting him, and then doing something else.

In later preschool (ages four to five) children's fears attach themselves more to alive objects such as barking dogs, big bad wolves, and monsters under the bed. These fears reflect your children's growing awareness of the big world out there, and how your child feels in relation to it.

Children of this age realize that grown-ups are big and powerful, and they are small and powerless, and we could hurt them. This is a God-given fear, because they need to be aware of other people and whether they are safe or not. Kids can even feel this way about their parents, even when the parent has not given the child cause to be fearful. To a child, every grown-up is ten feet tall.

Older preschoolers may also fear adults, large objects, animals, dark places, unfamiliar places, terrorists, Santa, bad people, demons, high places, sleeping alone (now that they know there are bad things out there, sleeping alone is way scarier). But remember, all these fears are really an outpouring of the central fear for this age: *"I am afraid of grown-ups because they are bigger and could hurt me."*

Children also have nightmares at this age. These are an attempt to work out these fears during their sleep.

For hints on how to help your children with nightmares, as well as all these fears, see *Things That Go Bump in the Night*, by Warren and Minirth.

Kids use play as the way they work through the many lessons they must learn. They cannot work out their fears by thinking them through rationally. They must do it through play. When we play with them, it shows them that adults won't overpower them.

When we allow them to be in charge of the play, it helps them see that they have some power too, rather than feeling powerless. There is often a correlation between how much they are played with and how fearful they are. The more play, the less fear, because they are able to resolve some of their fears through the process of playing.

Grade School: Six to Twelve

CHILDREN ENTER SCHOOL, begin to learn academically, and start to compare themselves to others.

The fears felt at these ages center around:

- I'm afraid I won't be as good as the other kids.
- I'm afraid I won't make it in life.
- I'm afraid I will lose the approval of those important to me, such as my parents, peers, and other important adults.

Sometimes these fears are expressed as:

- School avoidance: I'm afraid I can't be successful in this new situation.
- School phobia: I'm afraid to leave Mom and Dad. The real dynamic here is separation from home.

Kids work out their fears through competitive play, such as through board games, Little League, computer games, or physical challenges. They need to experience and prove they can succeed. They need a balance of free time and structured time so they have time to play out their fears.

One of the healthy lessons kids can learn at this stage is that *"I am of worth and value."* We want to teach our kids that a person's worth is not determined by what they do or how well they do it. Instead, a person's worth is determined by who that person is—a child of God who is deeply and immeasurably loved by God. When this fear is not resolved, it can persist into adulthood where the person never feels good enough.

Teenagers: Thirteen to Eighteen

TEENS ARE MOVING from the dependence of childhood to the independence of adulthood. It is not always a smooth transition. Your teens may not let you know they are fearful of all the changes, but they are.

Teens Between Thirteen to Fifteen Typically Have the Following Fears:

- I'm afraid of growing up.
- I'm fearful because I'm changing, and my parents are a mess and don't know much.

Later Teens (Sixteen to Eighteen) Are Mixed Up about Approaching Adulthood

THEY MAY VERBALIZE excitement about the benefits of their age (driving, later curfews, approaching the freedom of graduation and college). They are also experiencing fears about their future. Some of the common fears for this age are:

- I'm afraid of what I'm getting into (life).
- I'm afraid to cut the cord and go off on my own. I may not make it.

It is rare that teens will be able to recognize or verbalize these fears, but they are there nonetheless.

As parents, we need to make sure we are giving our teens positive, hopeful messages about their future. Sometimes without knowing it we may give messages that we don't want them to grow up, or we will miss them horribly when they are gone. We may also give messages that we fear they won't be able to get a job or will be saddled with student loans.

We need to express confidence in them and their future. It's normal for us to struggle with letting them go. We need to take care of our own feelings by talking with our spouse, friends, or a counselor.

It's not too late to help our children mature in their ability to process anger and fear. We can make a huge positive impact on our children in these areas.

Don't worry if you feel inadequate right now. It's never too late to learn how to process your own emotions and help your children.

God will help you know where to start. Ask Him for guidance. Don't be afraid to ask for help from friends, your pastor, a support group, or professional counseling. The efforts you make with your children in these areas will affect them positively for their entire life...socially, spiritually, relationally, and academically.

Now What? Where Do I Start?

Pray and ask God for His guidance and ask yourself some important questions:

1. What was most impactful for me in this chapter?
2. Where do I want to start (working on my own anger or fears, working with my children's anger, or working with my children's fears)?
3. What will be my biggest challenge with my children and myself?
4. What kind of support do I need from God and others?
5. Speak to yourself with compassion. *"This chapter hit me between the eyes. I didn't realize that my own issues with anger and fear were affecting how I interact with my children around these powerful emotions. It explains so much! I've never had help with these emotions, and I have been doing the best I could. I want to do better so I'm not struggling with these emotions myself and can help my children. I am a valuable person, and my emotions are good and placed in me by God. I'm going to learn how to process them without hurting myself or others. I think it will help me to get some help with all of this. I'm not bad because I struggle with anger and fear, I just haven't been taught how to regulate my own emotions and calm myself down. I don't have to do this on my own."*

10

Skills for Helping Kids Work through Tough Situations and Feelings

Shout for joy, you heavens; rejoice, you earth; burst into song, you mountains! For the Lord comforts his people and will have compassion on his afflicted ones.

Isaiah 49:13

CHILDREN NEED HELP dealing with the hard things of life. They have no idea how to handle their emotions or figure out what to do in difficult situations. Children experience hardships in a variety of ways—from a friend moving away or the loss of a pet to the death of a loved one. As life progresses, they may face other crises, such as divorce, bullying, the threat of terrorism, plus a whole lot more.

The principles shared in this chapter will help you build a closer relationship with your child as you help them adjust to whatever tough situations they are facing.

CRISES ARE UNAVOIDABLE

YOU CANNOT PROTECT your children or yourself from crises, no matter how hard you try. How we handle these tough situations and the resulting feelings affects our children, our relationship with them, and how we feel about ourselves as parents. These situations require skillful parenting, and how we handle these challenging situations really matters.

I love this quote by Karen Dockrey, in *When a Hug Won't Fix the Hurt*:

> *"It's OK to struggle—both as a parent and with your child. As you invite God along, He'll love you and equip your whole family to face what comes. God can understand because He has suffered. God can equip because He is all-powerful. God can give hope because He is Hope. God can give joy because no evil is strong enough to quench Him."*[20]

A crisis is an intense event or experience that overwhelms your system. It requires more than your emotional ability, maturity level, or coping skills can handle. The person who is going through the experience is the one who determines whether it is a crisis for him or her. Many factors go into why one experience may overwhelm one person but not another. These factors include age, emotional maturity, coping skills, past similar negative experiences, and personality makeup.

Some kids are susceptible to crises and don't handle them well. Other kids seem to roll with the punches. Some children come into the world with more anxiety than others, and they have a harder time adjusting to change in general. We need to be careful as parents to not look at difficult situations through our own eyes, but through the eyes of our child. It helps to factor in who they are, their temperament, and what they've been through. It's easy to look at a situation and think, *"This is not that big of a deal."* The reality is, for your child it may be a very big deal.

I made this mistake with my children when we moved and they had to change schools. I looked at it from my perspective. When I was in fifth grade, I had to go to a different school, and I don't remember it being that big of a deal. Unfortunately, this skewed my perspective when our children had to change schools when they were in fifth and seventh grades, respectively. I figured they would adjust easily, and I wasn't as sensitive to what an adjustment this was for them as I wish I'd been. It took me a few weeks to see things from their perspective and help them adjust in the ways they needed.

How We Handle Their Feelings Matters

IT MAKES A difference how we handle our children's feelings as they go through difficult times. Working through the immediate crisis is not all that's at stake. As they learn how to handle the death of a friend or dealing with a difficult teacher, they are learning coping skills that will benefit them for the rest of their lives.

It is normal when going through a crisis to experience lots of emotions and feel overwhelmed. When we treat their emotions seriously, they feel valued and that they matter. This also helps build a solid relationship with them and strengthens their character. The Bible is very clear that the primary way that builds character is through hardship. As our children weather hardships, they will grow in character.

> *And not only this, but we also exult in our tribulations, knowing that tribulation brings about perseverance; and perseverance, proven character; and*

> *proven character, hope; and hope does not disappoint, because the love of God has been poured out within our hearts through the Holy Spirit who was given to us.*
>
> Romans 5:3–5 (NASB)

As we come alongside our children during difficult times, it helps them not be alone in their struggles. There is a huge difference between going through a crisis alone or with someone supportive by your side.

Think about a past difficulty in your own life.

Was somebody there with you? Did someone support you emotionally? Did somebody care and take the time to listen? Did someone help you figure out what to do?

The answers to these questions makes all the difference in the world when going through difficult times. One of the reasons some people do better in a crisis is because they have support, while others do not. They may have been left to handle a situation they couldn't handle on their own.

Part of my work as a therapist was coming alongside others as they worked through painful memories of situations they originally had to handle by themselves. I was with them as they remembered these difficult experiences and felt painful emotions of long ago. This helped them get unstuck and let go of past crises that were weighing them down.

Perhaps the most important benefit of handling our children's emotions in healthy ways is that we model a caring and understanding God to them.

This is one of the scariest things about being a parent. The idea that I am a role model of God's love and care is frightening. It's a wonderful opportunity and a huge responsibility.

Why We Struggle with Handling Our Children's Emotions

IT IS VERY normal to have trouble knowing how to help our children deal with their emotions in healthy ways. There are lots of reasons why this is true.

- We may be not sure what to do. Most likely, no one ever taught us how to handle our emotions in healthy ways. It's hard to teach children skills that we were never taught.
- It is hard to tolerate and even welcome our children's pain. We want them to be happy, and we don't want them to go through hardships.
- On some level, we may think that if we explain the pain away by giving easy solutions or pat answers this will help them. Our desire may come from a very good place, but it doesn't help them. It benefits us, because we think we did something to help. Unfortunately, they feel even more alone when we do this.
- We may have been brought up to believe that when tough things happen you just tough it out and "pull yourself up by the bootstraps." This belief doesn't acknowledge the normal feelings that go with hard situations. God created the emotions they are experiencing for a reason, and they shouldn't be pushed aside.
- Trying to stay present and allow our children's pain may bring up unresolved pain from our past that we haven't worked through. Without meaning to, our natural reaction may be to push down our children's pain, just like we've done with our own.

PRINCIPLES FOR HELPINGS KIDS WITH THEIR FEELINGS

UNDERSTAND THE TRUTH ABOUT FEELINGS

AS WE'VE DISCUSSED in previous chapters, feelings are normal and God-given. They're not a mistake. God has no problem with the emotions we feel. He created emotions to guide us, enrich us, connect us, and to help us experience life more fully—in both the good and bad times. When going through a crisis it is normal to experience lots of strong emotions, such as anger, fear, hurt, confusion, and grief.

It is normal to feel deep grief about the loss of loved ones, relationships, health, purpose, dreams, or possessions. We need time to work through painful emotions. If we push these emotions away, they will resurface in physical, emotional, relational, and spiritual problems. There are no shortcuts to working through the losses of life.

When our children were teenagers, one of the boys in the youth group was killed in a car accident. It was very tragic and extremely difficult. I was so proud of our church. They held meetings for the teens where they could come and grieve and bond together. They provided grief counselors for them as well.

I worked with the parents of the teenagers attending to help them know how to help their children process their grief. There was a service to celebrate his life and also grieve his passing. They helped teens and their parents learn skills to grieve the loss of this young man. It was tragic and beautiful at the same time.

It's really important to not try to make your children take a shortcut to process their emotional pain. Believe me, I'm guilty of this too. We are vulnerable to do this because it is so painful to see our children suffer. It's easier to suffer yourself than watch your children suffer. Sometimes we shut down their emotions because it's so hard for us to see them in so much pain. It is necessary pain. God gives us grief to work through difficult times.

Children feel their feelings to the fullest in the moment. A small child can drop his cookie and scream in agony. The level of emotion that comes up is like a thousand on the Richter scale! Their emotions erupt, and they have no idea what is going on inside. They are still learning how to manage their feelings. When they come, they come.

When we minimize or deny our children's feelings, or focus on trying to "see the bright side," it makes their feelings get stuck inside and grow. When children's feelings are not expressed, they will act them out through anger, disobedience, or manipulation. They may also experience depression, anxiety, problems with concentration, or physical ailments.

By helping your children handle their emotions, you are giving them a gift more valuable than you could know. It is more valuable than anything you could buy them, or any place you could take them. Walking with them through the valley makes it possible to get to the other side, and it gives them skills they will use for a lifetime.

The core of most emotional and marital problems is the inability to feel, process, and express emotions in healthy and non-destructive ways. When we don't know how to process our emotions, they get played out in our future relationships. The work you are doing to help your children process difficult emotions will help them in their future friendships, marriage, work, and as a parent.

"Parents have trouble accepting our children's painful feelings because pain is hard. Our best efforts can't change the fact that anger, sadness, frustration, and fear are real. Whether we like them or not, sad emotions are normal and important feelings. God gave us these feelings for good rea-

sons...as children express their feelings, especially the scary ones, they gain the ability to handle them, and they discover what to do about them. When parents deny our children this privilege, we force them to suffer alone. We want a pain-free existence for our children. But pain is a part of life on this earth. Children hurt. Children want to talk about how they feel and what they think. Refuse to let your uneasiness or fear deny your children these very important needs."[21]

The listening and empathy skills that we learned throughout this book are the foundation of all that follows. Listening with your heart and mind for what it is like for your children to go through hard times is so important.

Get the Support You Need

WHEN YOUR CHILDREN go through a difficult time, you go through a difficult time. You may have been part of the same tragedy or impacted by how your children have been affected. Part of being there for your children includes being there for yourself. Try to make sure you eat as healthily as possible and get enough sleep. Let go of tasks or responsibilities that are not essential.

Getting support to navigate what you are going through is essential, and it will make this process a little easier. You aren't meant to go through this alone. You aren't supposed to know how to handle what's happened. Sometimes we expect ourselves to know how to help our children through a tragedy that we've never been through before. That makes no sense.

"Support" looks different for everyone. Give yourself permission to get help in the ways that work for you. Here are a few possibilities:

- Get information about the crisis through books, online searches, or getting information from others.
- Set aside some time alone to process your emotions while journaling, praying, walking, or resting.
- Talk with others who have gone through what you are going through. It helps to talk with others who truly understand, and they may have some important tips.
- Ask for a listening ear from others who will empathetically listen to your thoughts, feelings, and questions. This may come from your spouse, friends, family, support group, minister, or counselor.
- Seeking comfort and hope from Scripture, prayers, and music.
- Talk to yourself with kindness about what you are going through as you help your child.
- Take time to destress in whatever ways work for you, such as reading, massage, running, exercise, time in nature, and listening to music.

Taking care of yourself in the midst of your children's struggles helps you as well as your children. The better shape you're in, the more you'll be able to be there for your children. You deserve care and compassion too! Here are some questions to ask yourself that might help:

- What ways to be supportive to myself jumped out at me from the above list?
- What is one supportive thing I could do for myself this week?
- How has pulling in additional support helped me get through challenging times in the past?

Prepare Yourself

IF YOU KNOW your children have been through a difficult time, it helps to prepare yourself before an extended talk.

There may be lots of these talks over a period of time. Your love and presence is the most important thing you can do for your children.

First of all, pray.

Ask God for patience and courage to handle your children's feelings. Ask Him for empathy and understanding for your children, and wisdom to know what to do.

Pray that God will convey His love and acceptance through you to your children. Here are some tips to help:

- Plan a good time to talk. If possible, no interruptions. Smaller children might want to be held. Older children might want to talk while playing or taking a walk.
- Be a compassionate friend to yourself ahead of time. *"Take a deep breath. This is a chance to connect with my child in his pain. This is a chance to build our relationship. I'm not going to give pat answers, I'm going to try to be with him in the struggle."*
- Remind yourself that it is normal and natural for your children to be struggling with their emotions. It is not a sign of weakness or that something is wrong. Tell yourself, *"This is normal, it's what is supposed to happen. I'm glad I have this opportunity to help my children through this difficult time."*
- Call a friend and say, "I'm going to have a hard talk with Jimmy tonight, and I'm bringing up a tough issue. Could you please pray for me?"

HELP YOUR CHILDREN TELL THEIR STORY

WE WANT TO help our children talk about what happened, whether the crisis is small, medium, or large. Whether they got in trouble at school, have no friends, got in a car accident, or were mistreated in some way, they will need your compassionate help to tell their story.

Remember the larger goal. It's not just about getting the facts of the story.

It's about building a safe and caring relationship with your children in the process. It's about getting them to open up to you while they are in pain so they can receive comfort, understanding, and help.

REALIZE THERE ARE DIFFERENT WAYS TO TELL A STORY

1. Telling Their Story through Talking

Asking a lot of open-ended questions helps them share what happened. Realize they may only be able to share a little bit at a time, and that's okay. Be willing to mostly listen and empathize. Try to not interrupt, and ask good questions to help your children keep sharing.

- "Is there more?"
- "And then what happened?"
- "What was the hardest part?"
- "How are you doing?"
- "Are you okay?"
- "How were you feeling when she said that?"
- "What do you need right now?"

Try to not be discouraged if they don't have many answers. Your children may not be able to tell you verbally when they don't want you to ask any more questions. Set up a signal ahead of time so they can let you know.

"I'd like to ask you a few questions so I can understand what you went through and help you talk about what happened. I'm afraid I may not know when you want me to stop talking, so I'm wondering if you can wave your hand when you're done answering questions. Would that be okay?"

We want to help our children tell their story, so they can verbalize what happened and not be alone in it. We also want to know what happened. Try to be sensitive to how much they can share, and focus on empathizing with each piece they tell you.

2. Telling Their Story through Drawing

Many people, including adults, have trouble putting their feelings into words. As a therapist, I often asked children and teens to tell me what happened through drawing.

Ask: *"Can you show me what happened on this paper? Could you draw for me what your anger/fear/embarrassment looks like?"*

After: *"Tell me about your picture."* Don't assume you know what it means…listen to what your children say about each part.

Give simple input: *"Boy, you are angry... That must have been hard... I wish your friend didn't do that."*

It can also be helpful to draw a series of pictures, especially when there has been a death or traumatic event. Let's say your eight-year-old son's pet passed away. He's never experienced the grief of having a pet or anyone else he knows die.

It can be helpful to have him draw a series of pictures that expresses his emotions.

- Draw a picture of you and Pookie together. Ask, "What it was like to have him as a pet? What did you love about him?"
- Draw a picture of when you found out Pookie died. Ask, "What's it like now without Pookie? What do you miss the most?"
- Draw a picture of Pookie in heaven. "What do you need right now? How can I help?"

If your child asks, *"Will I see Pookie in heaven?"* It's okay to say, *"Yes."*

No one knows if there will be pets in heaven, and this is no time to go into a theological discussion about this. Your child will receive some comfort from this answer, which may very well be true.

3. Telling Their Story through Play

Children can use toys to show you what happened. As a therapist, it is common to use play to help children process their feelings. You don't need to be a play therapist to help your kids at home. They can use toys to show you what happened.

Let's say your child was in a car accident. It's nice to have toys that were part of what happened (for example, cars, ambulance, police car, doctors, etc.), but it's not necessary. Kids will use whatever is around.

Say, *"Show me what happened."* Realize it is normal and good for them to act out what happened to them. They are using play to act out and master whatever happened. It's just like an adult who talks, cries, or complains about something that is painful over and over again.

After 9/11, many children were traumatized personally or vicariously by watching reports on TV over and over. They took blocks and built two block towers and knocked them down, over and over—hundreds of times. It was their way of acting out what had happened. Don't be surprised if they act out what happened to them over and over again. It's not a bad thing, and it doesn't mean they're stuck. Sometimes it takes lots of repetition to master what happened.

DON'T WORRY IF YOUR CHILDREN OR TEENS REFUSE TO TELL THEIR STORY IN THE ABOVE OR OTHER WAYS

THIS IS FRUSTRATING but normal, much like when we don't feel like talking. If you ask to talk, and they say *no* or don't respond, say, *"That's okay, you must not be ready to talk and/or show me yet. I'm willing to listen when you are ready."*

Having difficulty sharing may be more about them trying to manage their pain, rather than a rejection of you, which is what it feels like. This is especially true with teenagers, as they try to handle more on their own. Here's advice from one of my son's teenage friends many years ago:

Kim: "What is it like when your parents try to get you to talk and you don't want to?"

Teen: "Oh, it's horrible, horrible…it's the worst thing."

Kim: "What's your advice?"

Teen: "Don't dig for info over and over. It feels like they don't hear you, and it feels violating to have someone go for information over and over when I said I don't want to talk about it. I'm not ready to talk about it. I'm either embarrassed or I don't want to think about it. You want me to deal with it. I don't feel like dealing with it. If you keep pushing, I won't listen to you anyway."

Kim: "Anything else?"

Teen: "Let some time pass and wait a while, and then you can ask me again."

Maybe wait a few days and try again. Ask gently and tentatively. They are more likely to own up to being *"a little bothered"* or *"kind of bugged"* or *"a little sad,"* than *"Did any huge, horrible thing happen at school you haven't told me?"* They're not going to tell you that. Here are a few options of how to ask them for additional information:

- "Hey. I know the other day it seemed like you were having a hard time when I asked about your friend. Are you doing okay?"
- "Is there anything going on with your friends that is bothering you a little bit?"
- "I asked if we could talk about what happened at school a few days ago, and it wasn't a good time. I really understand that, because sometimes I just don't want to deal with things. Would now be okay, or later today? Just so you know, it's not because I want to get down on you. I just want to know how you're doing, and if you're okay on the inside."

This may help your teens know they aren't in trouble or going to be interrogated. You might have to ask several times before the answer is yes. This gentle prodding helps them know they aren't alone, and that you are there to help. It keeps the door open. I often hung out near my teens and read magazines, and they would often just open up on their own.

Help Your Children Identify the Feelings Underneath the Words

REMEMBER THAT WHAT your children or teens initially share is only part of the story. This is because they are young and don't have a grasp on their emotions, or know how to communicate them. They don't leave out details to be deceptive. They leave them out because they are afraid of their own emotions, of our reaction, and of the situation itself. We get the *Reader's Digest* version because it's hard for them to share the whole story.

Important Things to Remember:

- Whenever your children express anger, there are other feelings under the surface that have yet to be expressed. What many people don't realize is that anger is a secondary emotion. What does this mean? Typically, one of the primary emotions, like fear or sadness, can be found underneath the anger. When angry, your children feel hurt or dismissed in some way. They may also feel afraid. So whenever your children or teens express anger, remember that they may also be feeling other emotions that need to be addressed as well.

Fear tells us we are afraid we are about to be harmed, and it includes anxiety and worry. Underneath the fear they may be feeling guilt or panic.

Sadness tells us we've lost someone or something important to us. Sadness comes from the experience of loss, disappointment, or discouragement.

Loneliness tells us we feel alone, or it may trigger deep feelings of abandonment from the past.

Fear and sadness can make us feel vulnerable and out of control. This is uncomfortable for most people, so people may avoid these feelings in any way possible. Parents and children alike may subconsciously shift into anger mode instead. Anger provides a surge of energy and makes you feel more in charge, rather than feeling vulnerable or helpless.

This is very important to know as a parent, so we can have compassion for our children. When they are angry, remind yourself that underneath that anger is a lot of pain, hurt, and fear. We need to have compassion for ourselves in this regard as well.

- Children and teens often share emotions and concerns at night. It is normal, although challenging for parents, when this happens. It may feel like they are doing this just to annoy you! Sometimes I felt like, *"I'm tired, I want to go to bed, and you want to talk. I was with you for six hours when we could've had a deep, meaningful conversation. Now I'm sleepy, and you want to talk."* At the same time, I was so glad to have these important conversations.

Let me explain why this happens. It's not personal. They share their emotions late at night because the worries, pain, and hurt from the day rises to the surface.

When kids are younger, we often have more time to talk with them. When they're teens, they're out and about, and the times available to talk are fewer and often at night. You have to deal with it. Parents of teens often get a lot less sleep.

- When children express their feelings, especially the tough ones, it is an invitation for us to help them, not to manipulate us. Feelings may come up when you're doing a project together or playing.

Some good questions to ask: *"How are you doing on the inside? Is there anything bothering you / hurting on the inside / you've been wondering about? How are you feeling about _________? How are you feeling about the football team? How are you feeling about your new teacher? Are there any kids at school you avoid?"*

We need to express empathy for our children in their struggles. Ask yourself: *"What would it be like to be my child in that situation?"* not *"What would it be like to be me in that situation?"*

Think about who they are as a person, what they've been through, and what their temperament is like.

Reflect back their feelings in an empathetic way. Let them know you heard them and the depth of their pain. Say, *"Oh, that was really hard for you. You were really afraid / embarrassed / sad / angry. You wish that had never happened. You are really struggling right now. You wish your friend treated you fairly."*

When kids tell us a tough story and are met with a listening ear and empathy, their feelings become more manageable. They don't feel so alone in their pain and are able to calm down more quickly. When they feel connected to you emotionally, they will feel safer with their emotions and want to share them with you.

Process Your Feelings about What Happened with Another Adult

IT IS NORMAL for you to have strong feelings of your own when you hear how your child is suffering.

It's fine to say to your child, *"I'm so angry she said that to you. I'm so sad that you went through that."* What we want to avoid doing is shifting the conversation to our distress by venting our anger or sharing our fears about how this may impact our child in the future. This isn't helpful to your child.

I've talked with many children who opened up to their parents and ended up having to comfort their parents rather than be comforted themselves. Your feelings, and the need to process them, are normal. They just need to be processed with your spouse, friend, or counselor, rather than your child.

BE HONEST ABOUT THE HARD QUESTIONS...

DON'T GIVE AN untrue answer or make promises that you can't keep. We need to address our children's fears and pain honestly, so that we can give them answers and skills to deal with the realities of life.

If they ask, *"Is Grandpa going to die?"*

Don't say no, if you think he might. Say, *"We don't know. I really hope not. I know it is scary to think of that happening."*

When hard things happen, it's normal to ask, *"Why did God let that happen?"*

They may be mad at God or question their faith. This is normal. Even adults ask these types of questions when faced with tragedy. Be honest about the hard questions, don't try to sugarcoat things. Make sure what you share is appropriate for their age level.

The reality is that we don't have answers for lots of their questions. We do the best we can.

What they need is for us to listen, care, and empathize as they ask the tough questions. An excellent faith-based book to find age-appropriate words to share with your children is *When a Hug Won't Fix the Hurt* by Karen Dockrey.

Sometimes suffering happens as a result of sin or the mistakes we made (1 Peter 4:15). That type of suffering is easier to take because at least there is an explanation for it.

The types of crises or hardships we have the hardest time with are when innocent people suffer through no fault of their own. These tragedies make no sense and seem so unjust.

Phil Yancey addresses these difficult questions in his book *Where is God When it Hurts?* He suggests that some people suffer for reasons we will not know until heaven. God doesn't always help us understand why He didn't intervene to stop a life-altering crisis. Instead, He points us to Himself for understanding, comfort, and the strength to get through it somehow.

I have wrestled with this question myself, as I deal with having a terminal illness. I take comfort in knowing that God is using my journey to help others. I know my suffering is not wasted. I don't understand it, but I trust God, and He has me in the palm of His hand.

I began this book as a way to help my adult children with the challenges of parenting. I knew I wouldn't be around to hold my grandbabies and help my children raise them.

I decided to write this book as a way of having a positive influence in their lives. Originally it was only going to be for them. As I wrote, I thought others might benefit as well. I pray that God will bless those who read it.

Going through crises and hardships can cause us to grow in our faith, as a person, and in our ability to empathize and love others. The challenge for ourselves and our children is to not become bitter or hardened by suffering, or reject God. He welcomes our anger, grief, and questions.

He can handle them, and He wants to help us get through what life has dealt us. Protect your heart as you go through difficult times.

Equip Your Children to Handle the Tough Situation or Pain

SOMETIMES A TRAGEDY has happened that can't be undone. You can be there to process it with them, but there's nothing that will change their reality. In these cases, you listen and provide comfort and support. Don't hesitate to get them help from a professional counselor to deal with the tragedy. In my experience, most parents wait too long. They hope their children's feelings will resolve on their own, which may or may not happen. As a parent and therapist, I encourage you to err on the side of getting them help earlier than later. No matter what, there are things you can do to help your children now.

Listen and Help Them Figure Out What to Do Next

THERE ARE LOTS of ways to help them think through what can be done to help their difficult situation. One important hint. When my kids came to me with a problem, I found that I was not good at guessing whether they just wanted a listening ear, or whether they wanted me to help them figure out what to do. After lots of incorrect guessing, I finally figured out to ask them, *"Is this something you want me to help you with, or is this a time when you want me to listen?"* They always knew the right answer, depending upon the situation,

"I want you to help me figure out what to do," or *"I just want you to listen. Don't tell me anything."* I really like asking them what they need rather than guessing. My guess rate is only 50 percent, so ask away!

Listen carefully to the problem and help them brainstorm possibilities. Share your ideas this way:

"Well, some kids in your situation might call their friend and see if she's okay, wait to see how things are tomorrow, or decide it's no big deal. What do you think?"

"Some kids want to visit their new school the first day, other kids just want to show up and wing it, or something in between. What do you think?"

It's good to offer possibilities for them to think about, so they can be involved in the solution.

- Anticipate with your children what hard times might be coming.
- Usually, whatever they are facing is brand new; something they've never been through before. They don't know what to do, and they are jumbled up inside emotionally. They can't anticipate the difficult challenges that lie ahead. Here are some examples:
    - The first time going back to school after a really hard incident.
    - The first time visiting the other parent after a separation or divorce.
    - The anniversary of a tragic event.
    - Your son was just diagnosed with type 1 diabetes and has to face a huge life change.

As you think about what they are facing, ask yourself, *"What would it be like to be my child in this situation?"* This will help you anticipate their needs. As you try to put yourself in their situation, try to think about what might be especially hard for them right now, and ask them about it.

- *"How do you feel about going back to school? What will be the hardest part?"*

- *"I know this is the first time going to Mom's new house. How are you feeling about going? Is there anything you need?"*
- *"How are you feeling as we get closer to the anniversary of the car accident? What can I do to help?"*
- *"I know the doctor gave you terrible news. I'd like to listen to how you're doing."*

Work with Your Children to Come up with Solutions

Ask: *"What might make this situation a little easier…before? during? after?"* Every child is different, and what they need in that situation may be different from what you would need. It's fine to give ideas, but follow their suggestions.

I remember when I was scheduled for back surgery and knew I'd be in the hospital for four days. I asked my ten-year-old daughter, *"What could help you while I'm in the hospital?"* She said, *"Can I wear one of your big shirts?"* I said, *"Of course. Let's go pick them."* So she picked out four big shirts, and she wore one every day. That's how she felt connected to me. I would've never thought of that. That was her solution.

Offer Hope

THIS STEP IS always offered after the previous ones. If you jump in straight to hope, your children will feel like you are "sugar-coating" their pain and they won't be able to take in the encouragement you have to offer. Resist the urge to give them hope right away.

They need to know you "get" their pain and feel emotionally close to you first.

When your children are in the middle of their suffering, it feels like it will go on forever. We can look at their situation with perspective, and realize that next year at this time, they will feel so much better. But they can't. They don't have the life experience and the emotional maturity to do this. They literally think they will feel this way forever. Once they know we understand what they are going through, they can take in some hope and perspective from us. Here are some examples:

Getting a shot: *"Yes, the shot will hurt at first, then it will feel much better, especially after we get ice cream on the way home."*

After a relative or friend dies: *"Yes, we will always miss John. It will hurt very badly for a while, then there will be short times when we won't think about it. Eventually we will feel happy again. He will always be precious to us and have a place in our hearts."*

Your child may say, *"No, no, no! I'm not going to feel happy again."* You respond, *"I know. Right now, you can't even imagine it, but maybe you could just borrow a little bit of my hope that eventually you won't feel as sad."*

It's okay if your children can't believe it. Later on, they will feel better.

Loss of a friendship: *"Yes, this is a very hard time. You probably won't be able to imagine ever being as good a friend with someone else as you were with Mary. But eventually you will have other good friends."*

Be prepared that they will insist they will never have as good a friend again. That's fine, that's part of their grieving process.

Loss of a pet: *"Yes, Sam is dead, and I'm very sad too. Let's sit here together and talk about all the things we loved about Sam. Let's draw a picture of you and him together. I'll be here to get you through this. After a while it won't hurt quite as much."*

Other creative ideas include making a slideshow of the pet, or creating a poster, or listing on paper all the things you loved about this precious pet. Don't just say, *"Let's go and buy another cat/dog."*

When our daughter was twelve, a cat we loved had heart problems and passed away. She made a website to tell people about her wonderful cat that passed away. I didn't even know she did it. She put pictures of him up there and emailed everybody she knew, to let them know that her cat had died. She included a link to the website so they could visit it. It was so cool. I had nothing to do with that, and learned about it when I got the email.

It's Not Too Late

IT'S NOT TOO late to revisit an old crisis with your children. You can be blunt and say, "I was just reading about how to help your children when they go through really hard times. It made me think about when you… I know it happened a while ago, but I wanted to check in and see how you are doing?" See if they are open to talk. If yes, you can ask questions like, "Do you still think about it? When does it come up? How has it gotten better? What still bothers you?" You can then be empathetic about what they shared and let them know how sorry you are that this happened. You can also ask if they need anything now. It's not too late. Your children will be touched that you care enough to ask at a later date.

When Your Children Need Extra Help

IT IS COMMON for parents to wonder whether their children's emotional problems are of the ordinary sort (likely to resolve on their own with family support) or more serious (requiring outside help).

If you've tried the skills shared throughout this book, and your child is still withdrawn, worried, stressed, tearful, or has behavioral problems, consider getting outside help from a trained therapist who specializes in treating children.

If your child has gone through a traumatic event, and is still having trouble coping, h/she may have developed post-traumatic stress disorder (PTSD). Not everyone who goes through a traumatic event will get PTSD. The chances of developing it and how severe it is varies based on things like personality, history of mental health issues, social support, family history, childhood experiences, current stress levels, and the nature of the traumatic event. Ask your doctor or a trusted friend for a referral to a therapist specifically trained in trauma therapy who works with children.

Now What? Where Do I Start?

1. Ask God for wisdom to help you to figure out where to start with each child. Ask Him to give you a sensitivity to what they are going through, and to show you how you might help. Think about a crisis that is currently happening in your child's life. How would you like to respond differently than you have before?
2. As you think about talking to your children about a really hard topic, ask yourself some important questions:
    - What am I already doing well in this area?
    - What is my first reaction when my child comes to me in a crisis?
    - Am I able to empathize? Do I want to jump in and fix it? When is it easier? Harder?
3. What did you learn in this chapter that you'd like to try out?

4. Are there issues my child is dealing with that are hard for me because of similar unresolved pain in my past? If so, consider getting help to resolve your issues so you can better help your children through their difficult times.
5. Speak to yourself with compassion. *"It is so painful to see my child suffer. I don't know how to help her. I wish this had never happened and she never had to go through this. I feel so helpless, even though I'm doing a lot to help her. I want to be kind to myself and get the support I need. It's helping to talk to my friend, and I'm making sure I get some exercise. I'm going to stop telling myself I should be doing more. The truth is that I'm doing a lot, and being with her through this difficult time is giving her much-needed support. I will continue to pray that God gives both of us the strength we need to walk through this difficult time."*

11

Family Skill Building: Chores, Allowance, and Family Meetings

Bear with each other and forgive one another if any of you has a grievance against someone. Forgive as the Lord forgave you.

Colossians 3:13

ESTABLISHING STRUCTURE AROUND chores, homework, allowance, and family meetings is very important because it helps busy parents and teaches children skills they need. We live complicated lives, and establishing predictable routines helps so much. It helps to lower stress, creates stability rather than chaos, and makes time to enjoy one another, rather than always putting out fires.

Establishing Family Routines Helps Our Kids

HELPING OUR CHILDREN develop life skills such as how to handle money, do household chores, negotiate for what they want, and complete difficult tasks helps them mature as a person.

It also gives them the skills they need in the future, and develops their character.

A person's character largely determines how they will succeed in life, both in work and in interpersonal relationships. Most of the problems people have result from character weaknesses. A major part of successful parenting is helping children develop a strong moral character. This increases the chances that their future will go well.

DEFINITION OF "CHARACTER"

"The word character *means different things to different people. Some people use character to mean moral functioning or integrity. We use the word to describe a person's entire makeup, who he is. Character refers to a person's ability and inability, his moral makeup, his functioning in relationships, and how he does tasks. What does he do in certain situations, and how does he do it? When he needs to perform, how will he meet those demands? Can he love? Can he be responsible? Can he have empathy for others? Can he develop his talents? Can he solve problems? Can he deal with failure? How does he reflect the image of God? These are a few of the issues that define character."*[22]

As we teach them important life skills, we need to keep in mind the big picture, which is the development of their character.

TEACHING LIFE SKILLS

IT'S IMPORTANT TO distinguish between life skills and chores. Life skills are abilities you want your children to learn before they leave home. These include things like managing money, doing laundry, basic cooking and cleaning, decision-making skills, and time management. Children also benefit from people skills such as basic manners, respect for elders, being a good listener, empathizing, and resolving conflict.

Part of parenting involves teaching our children life skills. If we can't, we help our children learn them from someone else. For instance, let's say you'd like your child to learn how to sew but don't know how to yourself. Enrolling you both in a class and learning together would be a solution. You can also collaborate with other parents to teach your children life skills. One parent may show how to plant a garden, and one may demonstrate how to manage finances. None of us know how to do everything, and teaching them life skills doesn't have to happen all at once.

Some parents use summer to teach life skills because the school year is so busy. As children learn, we praise them for their progress and provide logical consequences to teach them when they do not follow through.

Combining instruction with love and grace can build relationships with your children, build their self-confidence, and develop their character. Teaching these skills prepares them for a successful future.

Tips for Chores

For even when we were with you,
we gave you this rule: "The one who is
unwilling to work shall not eat."

2 Thessalonians 3:10

THE BIBLE IS clear throughout Scripture that everyone works and contributes, unless they are truly unable to. It is very important for our children to participate in running our households. We are not there to serve them. Being part of a family is important practice for learning to serve and receive in a group. They need to become skilled in running a household, working together as a team, and persevering through tasks.

Chores are ongoing tasks that benefit your family and household. There is a lot that goes into running a home. When children aren't involved in doing chores, they may think that food, clean clothes, and a kept yard just happen.

Don't worry if you don't have a system for having your children consistently help with chores yet. You can start a little bit at a time. Remember to extend compassion to your children as you teach them new skills they may not want to learn. Be compassionate with yourself as set up and enforce chores for your children. We are all on a learning curve, and no one will do it perfectly.

Kids model what we do, not what we say. Do they see us keeping up with our chores? Do they see us have a positive attitude about it? Do they see us express satisfaction at how good it feels to get them done? Do they see us do a good job? Do they see us do the hard stuff before the fun stuff?

When our children see us do our chores with a mostly positive attitude, it will help them see chores as a normal part of life.

It's Normal to Face Resistance

IT IS TYPICAL for kids to not want to do chores. I don't really like to do them either. Allow them to struggle with not wanting to do their chores, while still doing them. This is part of growing and maturing as a person. Here's something you might say,

> *"I know you don't want to do your chores before you go to Emily's. I know just how that feels. That is still what will need to happen, and I am happy to drive you over to her house when they are completed."*

This communicates compassion for how hard it is to do things we're not happy about, while still having to do them. This is a part of adulthood I'm not crazy about myself.

Expect a Learning Curve

KIDS HAVE TO be taught how to do everything. They need to have the freedom to fail and learn from their mistakes. Children benefit from instruction without shame.

Instruction says, *"You did a great job sweeping the floor. The job will be finished when the broom is put away."*

Shame says, *"What's wrong with you? Don't you even care enough to finish the job? Put that broom away, NOW!"*

Don't pass judgment or criticize their performance as they learn. There is a steep learning curve for anyone when learning to master a chore.

Comment on the positives, *"Wow, you folded all those clothes,"* rather than pointing out the parts that aren't quite right, like putting the clothes in the wrong piles. Being criticized while learning can be very discouraging, and will stop them from wanting to help and learn.

Imagine this: your six-year-old wants to help you sweep the floor. Now the honest truth is that kids are horrible when they first learn to sweep the floor. All they really do is push the dirt, fish crackers, and who knows what else from one side of the room to the other!

We need to keep in mind that this is not really about teaching sweeping.

That's a small part.

It's more about giving them the message that they:

- are a good worker;
- are able to learn new things;

- have a wonderful desire to help; and
- are making a good effort.

These learning experiences contributes to their overall self-esteem of being a valuable and capable person. This is actually what teaching them to do new things is about…not whether they missed a spot or not.

Talk to Yourself with Compassion

CHILDREN BEGIN DOING "chores" by imitating us. They want to do what we're doing. They rarely decrease our workload, and usually increase it! We want to focus on encouraging their desire to help, and complimenting them for their efforts. With time, they will master the skills.

If you get frustrated, talk to yourself compassionately the way I do.

"This isn't helping, I'm going to have to do this all over. Okay, take a deep breath, this isn't about helping me make cookies. It's about giving her messages that she is capable, can learn new things, is a good helper, and feels encouraged by me. Hang in there, remember the big picture."

Talk to Your Children with Compassion

EXPLAIN THAT MISTAKES are normal. Many of us spend a lot of our lives trying to be perfect, never make mistakes, or not admit mistakes we've made. Our culture, media, and distorted views of our faith support this belief system.

To pursue this impossible goal, we've got to believe a whole bunch of things that aren't true:

- That perfection is possible…it isn't.
- That if we pretend to be perfect, we are…not!
- That others will like us more if we are perfect. Some might, but for most, appearing perfect makes us impossible to relate to or get close to.
- That "perfection" on the outside means we're okay on the inside…the opposite is usually true.
- That mistakes are bad…they're not. They're just a normal part of learning.
- That we can't survive the shame we feel when a mistake is exposed…not true, forgiveness by God and self-compassion can soothe the pain and regret we feel.
- That covering up mistakes is the way to go. Not so. Often admission of them brings healing, repair of relational damage, and renewed trust.

Our children as well ourselves need to hear regular messages like this:

- "It's normal to make mistakes, everyone does."
- "You are loveable no matter what."
- "It's normal to not know how to make your bed at first. You'll learn a little at a time."
- "Mistakes are necessary, it's how we learn."
- "Yes, you'll feel bad because you didn't get it quite right. You can learn from it and feel better again."
- "God loves you completely, warts and all. There's nothing you can do to make God love you less."
- "I love you as you are. There's nothing you can do to make me love you less."

Distinguish Between Perfectionism and Striving for Excellence

WE SOMETIME CONFUSE perfectionism with striving for excellence. It's important for us to be clear about this, both for ourselves and our children. Healthy striving for excellence means giving whatever we're doing our best shot, so we can feel good about what we've accomplished. Healthy striving is internally driven. It's about setting a goal that is important to me, and giving it my all.

This is very different than striving for perfection. Perfectionism is all about *"What will people think?"* and is externally driven. We are on a quest to be perfect, so we can avoid or minimize feeling shame, blame, and judgment. This cycle is addictive as we strive to be good enough, which never comes.

If you struggle with perfectionism, no doubt you don't want to pass this unhealthy striving onto your children. Perfectionism is contagious, and we cannot raise children who are more resilient to perfectionism than what we are.

The good news is that as we work on practicing self-compassion, we can begin to slowly heal our perfectionism. We can learn to embrace our limitations, forgive ourselves, and let go of mistakes. Our children will see us being nonjudgmental toward ourselves while still striving for excellence. This will help them handle their mistakes more easily, which is especially important as they tackle doing chores on a regular basis.

Chores According to Age

AS YOU THINK about what chores to have your children do, it's good to ask yourself these two questions. *What chores are im-*

portant for my children to learn? and *What are they capable of doing?*

The following are just a few suggestions. There are many more ways your children can help. You will have a different list that fit your child or life situation.

Here are some ideas to consider:

Two to three-year-olds can assist you in chores you regularly do, such as helping you make the bed, pick up some toys, put their dirty clothes in the laundry basket, and dust.

Four to five-year-olds can wash their hands, pick up their toys, sort laundry, wipe off the counter, and set out clothes for the next day.

Six and seven-year-olds can be given simple tasks such as cleaning up messes they make, helping clean their rooms, make their beds (not strict standards), set the table, and water garden plants.

Eight to eleven-year-olds can unload the dishwasher, empty the trash, fold laundry, sweep, dust, scrub the sinks, take care of personal hygiene, make their lunches, be responsible for their homework, and take care of a pet.

Twelve and thirteen-year-olds can take care of personal hygiene, belongings, and homework, prepare a few simple meals with supervision, clean the bathroom and vacuum, do simple yard work, get themselves up with an alarm, and clean their room.

Fourteen and fifteen-year-olds can mow the lawn, wash windows with supervision, weed, do their laundry, and prepare a menu and grocery list.

Sixteen to eighteen-year-olds can get a part-time job or babysit, prepare meals, maintain the car they drive, and pay for a few of their expenses such as toiletries and entertainment.

How to Get Started

IF YOU WOULD like to begin chores with your kids, or renegotiate them, here are some tips that will help:

Frame chores as each of us "doing our fair share" as opposed to "helping" Mom and Dad. They need to see these chores as a normal part of contributing to the household.

Make a list of all the chores that need to be done to run the house. Write down everything you do for a week. Include everything, like working to earn money, paying the bills, driving family members to school and errands, going grocery shopping, etc. Post your list on the refrigerator, and ask others to add to the list of things they would like you to do for them. A few days later, have a family meeting to decide how to divide up the chores. Give your kids input into which chores they do. Assign appropriate to age and difficulty, and make sure each child get the same amount of easy and hard chores to do.

You'll need to decide if you'd like your children to do daily chores and/or weekly chores. Make it clear when their chores need to be done.

"You'll need to have your chores done by *Saturday at 4:00 p.m. before I drive you to your friend's house / before your next meal."*

Give a reasonable period of time to complete them, rather than demand they do them right now.

Once you've assigned chores, put a list on the refrigerator with each person's chores and when they need to be completed. See the chore list on the next page that was on my refrigerator at home when our kids were in junior high and high school.

Weekly Chores

Completed by 4:00 p.m. on Saturday; if spending the night at a friend's house, by 4:00 p.m. on Sunday

Son	Daughter
Empty dishwasher*	Empty dishwasher*
Put clean clothes away	Put clean clothes away
Empty cat box*	Empty cat box*
Mow grass (1 acre)	Fold 4 loads of laundry
Clean bathroom toilet and shower*	Clean bathroom sink*
Empty trash	Vacuum stairway

* These chores rotated. One week one child unloaded the top rack of the dishwasher, and the other one unloaded the bottom rack; then it switched the next week. Same with cleaning the bathroom and emptying the cat box. This way there weren't fights about who had to do the chore they both hated.

Daily Chores

Son	Daughter
Empty dishwasher*	Empty dishwasher*
Set table**	Set table**
Make lunch for the next day	Make lunch for the next day

* See above.

** One brought the plates and cups, one put out the napkins and silverware, and they switched who did what each week.

Having their chores structured and fair really cut down on fighting.

When They Don't Do Their Chores

WHEN THEY DON'T do their chores, ask if they would like to do them or pay out of their allowance to have someone else do them. If they have no money, you can either deduct the amount from next week's allowance or buy one of their toys to pay to have the chore done by someone else. Let them know they can buy it back later. This is what happens in the real world. If you don't have money, you sell some of your belongings.

It is very important to dole out consequences without anger. We are not punishing them, we are lovingly instructing them about consequences and responsibility. If we share consequences with anger, their focus comes off of themselves and their actions and refocuses on how "unfair" we are.

You can also offer your children the option to earn extra money by doing extra chores around the house. This may teach them that obtaining money takes work. It may also give them some financial freedom to save or to buy certain things they want. This can be empowering for kids and give them a sense of pride.

You can also be creative with other consequences that happen if chores aren't completed in time. Remember the real-life story I told back in chapter 6 about what happened after one of our children didn't complete their chores? Check it out. It only happened once.

Now What? Where Do I Start?

1. What do you think about this section on chores?
2. Do your children do chores regularly?
3. What is already going well?
4. What is working, and what needs adjusting?
5. What do you want to start adding or changing?

ALLOWANCE: TEACH YOUR CHILDREN THE VALUE OF A DOLLAR

WE LOVE TO see our kids happy. As a mom, I enjoyed buying my children toys and giving them special treats from time to time. I also wanted to teach them the value of a money, and how to manage it. This is a very important life skill. They only learn this skill through practice, not by being told what to do.

THE VALUE OF ALLOWANCE

THERE ARE MANY differing opinions about whether kids should be given an allowance or not. Some believe they shouldn't pay their kids for doing chores, and others say that giving an allowance is a good idea. I agree that children should not be paid for doing their fair share of chores around the house. The purpose of giving an allowance is to give them practice in handling money, just like we give them practice doing chores or learning to drive.

Here are some guidelines to get started:

Sit with your children and tell them that you want to help them learn how to handle money. If you have a value that saving and/or tithing (giving 10 percent of your money to God) is important, this is a great way to teach this to your children as well. Explain how you manage money in your own life—where you put savings and why, who you give your tithe to and why. If you help your children learn how to save and give now, it will become a habit, and will be much easier for them later in life. Here's something you might say,

"You've been learning so many important things like going to school and sweeping the floor. You are doing such a good job. We think you are ready to learn how to handle money. We work at our jobs to earn money. Some of the money pays for food, the

car, and our house. Some of it we put in the bank to save for later, like going on vacation, or when we need to buy a new washing machine. Some of it we give to our church each week to help people be close to God.

"Each Saturday we are going to give each of you 50 cents. We'd like you to save 5 cents in this envelope for something special in the future, and 5 cents to give when we go to church. You can put that in this special envelope. That leaves you 40 cents to spend or save for something important to you. You can keep this money in this special box you can decorate.

"There's a very important rule. Once you spend your 40 cents, it's gone until the next Saturday. If you spend it all on something Wednesday, you'll have to wait until Saturday for the next time we pass out allowance. Do you have any questions?"

We gave them a small amount of allowance to start. You can decide what amount is appropriate for you.

Practical Tips

ONCE CHILDREN REACH age five or six, give them a small allowance per week. Give it to them on the same day each week in an envelope. If they are getting 50 cents a week, and you want to encourage saving and giving, give it to them in dimensions that encourages this (four dimes and two nickels). Remember the purpose of the allowance is to give them the experience of handling money. You are not paying them to do chores.

Your children are allowed to spend the money as they'd like. The rule is that once the money is gone, it's gone until next payday. When your kids have spent their money, and complain that they have no money, you smile and say, *"That's hard, but don't worry...there will be more next Saturday."* This is a great chance for them to learn from their mistakes. It's the only way they will learn to save for things they want.

Don't take money away from your children when they don't do their chores. They can use some of their money to pay you or their siblings to do their chores if they don't do them. You can say, *"Would you rather clean up your room or hire me (or your brother) to do it for you?"* This actually replicates the real world. Grown-ups can use their money to pay others to do their tasks.

When you go shopping, your children can decide what they want to buy. If they spend it all on candy, you can decide how much they can have at a time and when. They will of course be shocked when their money runs out, but this is the way they will learn.

Giving your children an allowance so they get hands-on experience gives them skills handling money that will benefit them a lifetime. By doing this, you are encouraging independence and empowering them to make their own choices and learn from their mistakes. It is also gives you an easy way to talk about decision making as they decide how best to spend their money.

When our children got to be in junior high, we decided we wanted them to learn how to manage more money for a longer term. For two weeks, I wrote down all the money I spent on them. I kept track of things like renting one video game and one movie per week, two snacks at fast food per week, and various other costs.

I added it up and gave them this amount each week to make their purchases. It was amazing to watch them decide that spending their money to rent a video game wasn't worth it. It was fine when I was paying, but not when they were! When they asked me to buy them things, I referred them to their allowance.

In high school, we added money for clothes they had to factor in. They learned a lot about how to manage their own money and have great skills in this area as adults.

You can personalize this for your children and your unique situations. Many adults have difficulty handling money wisely because they weren't taught to do so when they were small. You have a chance to help your children in this area, and having these skills will make a difference in their lives!

Don't worry if you don't see yourself being skilled in these areas yourself. There are many ways you can learn too. There are some wonderful books out there that parents and children can read together to learn money management, such as *Smart Money, Smart Kids: Raising the Next Generation to Win with Money* or *Money Matters for Teens.* Please see the bibliography for more information.

Now What? Where Do I Start?

1. What stood out to you from this chapter?
2. What do you think of giving your children an allowance to help them learn how to manage money?
3. Would it help you to go through a book with your kids on managing money?
4. How would you like to bring this idea up for discussion?
5. Come up with a plan, and start small.

Family Meetings

GETTING TOGETHER REGULARLY as a family to connect, have fun, and handle family business is very important. These meetings provide a great opportunity for children to learn how to express their ideas, needs, and desires. It also gives them a place to negotiate, argue their point, and compromise as they learn to balance others' needs with their own.

Children feel valued when they are listened to, heard, and know that what they shared factors into decisions being made. It gives them a real-life experience that their thoughts, feelings, and needs matter too.

These family times give parents a chance to bring up items the family needs to think about regarding everyday issues, upcoming plans, or future decisions regarding vacations or other concerns This gives children important insight and experience into what it takes to run a household and nurture a family.

How Do They Work?

YOU CAN SHARE with family members (when already together) that we want to start to have a family time regularly where we can bring up concerns, encourage one another, and have fun together. Ask everyone how they feel about that. By asking this question, you've just started your first family meeting!

Decide together what each of you would like to happen or not happen at family meetings. Meetings won't be safe if they become a time to tattle on someone else or bring up a problem with one child in front of the other children. This should be done privately.

Meetings can be short (five to ten minutes) or longer, and consist of:

- Answering "get to know you" questions, such as, *What's the best/hardest part of* being five, ten, or being a grown-up? What's your favorite planet? What are you most proud of? What are you looking forward to this year? What is your biggest struggle right now?
- Problem solving.
- Future planning, such as "Where does everyone want to go on vacation?"
- Doing a project together.
- Reading the Bible together.
- Having fun, playing together.

Don't give into the temptation to bring up all sorts of issues that have been bothering you now that you have a captive audience. If you do, your family will dread these family meetings.

Family meetings can take a little time to set up, but they are so worth it. Remember the bigger goal: to build a safe place for family members to come and learn how to express themselves, negotiate and compromise, as well as have fun together. You will have good discussions such as,

"Yes, what you want is very important, and so is what your sister wants. Let's figure out a way that is good for both of you."

"How should we decide which games to play during our family meeting? We want to come up with a solution that gives everyone an equal say."

"It seems like our system for getting ready in the morning isn't working, because mornings seem so stressful. This is such a hard way to start the day. Let's talk about what we are doing now and some ideas that will make mornings easier."

We want to build an environment where everyone's needs are important, not just the most powerful, loud, or manipulative person. These types of interactions will benefit your children later in life, as they establish their careers, choose marriage partners, negotiate relationships, resolve conflict, and manage their homes.

Some Tips

START FAMILY MEETINGS with a prayer and an encouragement for each person (no qualifying compliments…this negates them). *"You did a great job picking up your room"* versus *"I was glad to see that you finally picked up that health hazard of a room."*

Be consistent. It is very important to follow through with these meetings. If we say we will meet every Friday night and don't, it will cause our children to not trust us and it will discourage their hearts. *"I thought we'd get together and I could say what's important to me, but I guess what I think and feel isn't important after all. I guess this is another one of those things Mom and Dad say they'll do but don't do."* Trust is built when we do what we say and are consistent. If once a week feels like too much to manage, try meeting every other week to start.

Family meetings can be followed by a family fun time if desired (reading a good book together, playing games, hiking, sports, or watching a movie).

These important meetings provide an opportunity to bring up concerns, connect, interact, negotiate, and enjoy one another. If a concern is brought up that you need time to think about before it is discussed, put it on the schedule for next time.

Ground Rules to Make Family Meetings Safe

THE FOLLOWING IS a sample you can personalize for your family.

You can come up with rules based on how family members answer the question, "We want our meetings to feel safe. What would each of you like to happen, or not have happen, at our family meetings?"

Once you've come up with a list, type it up and post in the room where you'll meet. This list can be amended as you go.

1. All members attend…even if they are not in the mood to share.
2. All members show respect for one another's feelings. This means no put-downs, name calling, hitting, or making fun of what each person brings up.
3. Each person speaks for themselves. No sharing what you think the other person is thinking or feeling.
4. Members listen to what each person is saying.

5. No giving unsolicited advice. No lectures, "shoulds," or "oughts."
6. It's okay to pass on sharing your opinion. This needs to be accepted and not shamed.

Normal Reactions to Expect:

FAMILY MEMBERS MAY be resistant to sharing their feelings. This can happen if personal sharing or opinions have been met in the past with shame, anger, put-downs, lectures, or *"I told you so."* If this happens, it's better to start with watching a funny TV show together, and then later add talking.

If that's the case, you will need to become a safe person to share with. You may not have known a healthier way before now and that's okay. We've talked a lot about healthy ways to communicate in prior chapters, so you are already on your way!

If someone doesn't want to share, say, *"That's okay, sometimes I don't want to either. If you change your mind, just let us know."* It's better for meetings to be short (ten to fifteen minutes), safe, and a success than long and a disaster.

Now What? Where Do I Start?

1. What do you think about having regular family meetings?
2. What do want to happen, and not happen, at your family meetings?
3. What types of topics would you like to bring up?
4. What are some fun things you can do during your family meetings?
5. What's an easy way to start?
6. What makes you nervous about starting family meetings?

Compassion for Parents

I KNOW THIS may feel like a lot to add to your already busy life. My experience is that setting up some structure around chores, allowance, and family meetings will actually reduce stress and increase closeness.

When things are chaotic, parents and children are stressed and feel like a failure. I have great compassion for how hard it is to start something new. I encourage you to set up systems that will lower your stress, reduce chaos, and teach your children life skills. It's much better than spending your precious time and energy putting out fires.

How about talking to yourself with compassion?

"Reading this chapter is exciting in one way, because it is wonderful to know there are things we can do to make out home run more smoothly while teaching the kids the things they need to know. I sure wish I'd been taught how to do this when I was a child. On the other hand, I feel bad that haven't set up these systems before. I want to be kind to myself. There's no way I could have known how to do any of this if I'd never been taught. I think I'll start small with the easiest thing and see how it goes. It's okay to make small steps."

12

Coaching Your Kids Through Life

When Jesus landed and saw a large crowd, he had compassion on them, because they were like sheep without a shepherd. So he began teaching them many things.

Mark 6:34

ONE OF THE powerful ways to influence your children is to come alongside them as their coach, encourager, and challenger. To do this we need hands-on skills to coach them through the challenges of life.

We want to bring out the best in our kids, as well as ourselves, as we parent from our personal and spiritual values.

As parents, we want to empower our kids to create their own internal motivation, acquire the skills and tools they need, and hold themselves accountable for moving forward.

When we think about the concept of "coaching" our kids, it's helpful to think about the kind of coach we want our kids to have when they are first learning a sport or new skill.

Qualities of a Good Coach

WE HAND OVER the instruction and encouragement of our children to others throughout their lives.

Whether your children are in band, on a sports team, in drama, or on another competitive team, every parent hopes their kids get a good coach. We all hope our kids will get "this" coach, instead of "that" coach.

You know what I mean. I was speaking a while back on this topic, and I asked the parents, "What are the qualities of a good coach?"

Here's what they said:

- Brings out my child's potential
- Understanding
- Makes learning fun
- Patient and kind
- Motivator
- Has integrity, a role model
- Help kids handle failure in a healthy way
- Encouraging
- Helps set goals
- Comfortable with trial and error
- Hopeful
- Inspiring
- Help see the big picture
- Focused on character development, not just outcome
- Cares about the welfare of my child
- Good listener
- Sets a good example

That's a pretty wonderful list. I definitely would want my kids to have a coach like that. These parents also let me know the kind of coach they did not want their kids to have.

- Shaming
- Impatient
- No time spent teaching
- Focus on results only
- Coaching is about the coach, not about the child
- Unwilling to listen
- Unable to see the big picture of character development
- Values obedience and compliance only
- Uncomfortable with trial and error
- Yelling
- Not in control of his/her emotions
- Sees my child as a tool to win

Whew! That is quite a list too. It makes my skin crawl to think of handing my children over to a coach like this. There is a lot of wisdom we can glean from these two lists as we contemplate being a positive coach in our children's lives.

What Does Being a Coach in Our Children's Lives Look Like?

BEING A COACH in our children's lives means coming alongside them in different roles as needed, depending upon their age, temperament, and who they are as a person. Some of the ways to influence them in compassionate ways includes being:

A Teacher

THIS MEANS TEACHING them what they need to know as they enter each new phase of life. They come into the world knowing nothing. They are like sponges, ready to soak up information, encouragement, love, and experiences.

Our challenge is to teach them in ways that don't make them feel stupid, because they are vulnerable sponges.

As mentioned in previous chapters, we do this by encouraging them for what they are doing right, normalize how normal failure is while learning, and grow from their mistakes. We teach them with a foundation of compassion that cushions their hearts and minds.

An Encourager

BEING A COACH in our children's lives means being an encourager to them, whether they're one, twenty, forty, or sixty. They continue to enter new phases of life while learning new things. They need and appreciate our encouragement throughout their lives.

We want to encourage them whenever they make good choices, show good character, or learn from their mistakes. Each of these positive choices encourages the development of their character.

Their character indicates who they are on the inside. Are they honest, patient, and kind; do they think about others as well as themselves; do they take care of themselves? Their character is primarily what determines their actions.

Anytime they show good character, we want to encourage them.

A Thought Provoker

AS THEY GROW, we guide them, helping them come up with their own ideas and motivation. We don't tell them what to do, but we guide them to what they need to consider. Our children grow and mature as we ask good questions to help them think through their decisions and choices. Their brains are not fully developed until between twenty-five to thirty. Asking our children good questions helps their brains develop, which aids them in making better decisions.

We want to help them learn how to think, not tell them what to think. It's very easy as a parent to jump in and tell them what to do. We've lived a lot of life, have been through tough situations, and have a lot of wisdom to share. It's hard to not jump in and tell them what to do, especially when we know they haven't thought things through. As much as we want to lay out exactly what they should do, it's not our job. Our job is to ask questions to get them to think about options and possible consequences, so they make wise decisions. Being a thought provoker requires a huge amount of self-control to not say everything you are thinking!

A Disciplinarian

STUDIES HAVE SHOWN that if kids get a lot of love and encouragement, they need a lot less discipline…which is always good news! Our discipline helps our children when we discipline with logical consequences, not shame. Here's an example:

I know a father who came up with a creative way to discipline his son for slamming his door. He told him twice to stop doing this, but he kept it up. He decided to come up with a different way to get his message across, rather than arguing, lecturing, or using shaming messages, such as, *"I'm so disappointed in you.*

You don't care about anybody but yourself. You have no respect for the great house I provide for you."

Instead, while his son was away, he went up his room with a drill and took the door off.

When his son came home he was shocked. His dad said, *"It's a privilege to have a door. You can't have one if you are going to slam it. You're going to lose your door for a while, and then we'll give you another chance to use your door appropriately."*

He could have shamed his son, but all that would have done is make his son feel awful, his dad feel powerless, and harm their relationship. No learning would have occurred.

When I was forty-eight, I got my first speeding ticket. When the police officer pulled me over, I didn't even contest it. He told me I could challenge my ticket in court. I said *"No, I was speeding."* To make matters worse, our sixteen-year-old daughter was with me. I wasn't a good example to her.

I went through traffic school online. It was horrible. The price of the ticket was bad enough, but having to do traffic school made me never speed again. It took me five hours to get through it, and I completed it on the last day possible. I was insufferable to be around and complained constantly. My family never wants me to speed again!

This was a logical consequence imposed by the State of California, and I learned. When I went home and told my husband, he could have given me a lecture about the insurance rates, the cost of the ticket, or that I wasn't being a good example to our daughter. He didn't. He let the logical consequence of going to traffic school do the teaching. And no, I haven't gotten a ticket since!

Logical consequences are powerful because this is how the real world works. When they don't do their homework, and get in trouble, it is a preview of what will happen at work. If they're consistently late or don't do what's assigned, they're going to lose their job.

Jesus is Our Example

HE USES MANY ways to help us learn. One of the ways is to give us free will, let us make mistakes, and hopefully have us learn from them. I did a study in the Gospels a number of years ago to observe how Jesus interacted with people. I wanted to see how He taught them, how He responded to their questions, as well as how He applied discipline.

Jesus taught His followers at large and small gatherings in a straightforward way, as well as through stories known as parables. When asked questions, sometimes He would answer directly, while other times He would respond with a question in return. When necessary, Jesus disciplined those whose hearts were hardened or had evil motives.

It was really enjoyable to learn about the powerful ways Jesus used to teach His dear children principles to live a wise and impactful life. Here's what I discovered:

Teacher

HE TAUGHT PRINCIPLES directly. He would spend time with his apostles, disciples, and followers and taught them about God, life, and following Him. As you read the Gospels there are many examples of this.

This is a good model for us. Jesus taught His disciples and followers what He felt they needed to know and corrected their beliefs as needed. Part of our job is to teach our children what they need to know, and correct their false views of the world.

Thought Provoker

JESUS WOULD ACT as a thought provoker by asking questions to get them to think. As you read the Gospels you will be shocked at how many questions He asked. Here are a few examples from the book of Matthew: 9:1–7; 12:1–8; 12:22–37; 15:1–9, 10–20; 16:5–12; and 20:20–28.

1. He answered questions with questions to get them to think.

In Matthew 12:22–28, He says,

> *Then they brought him a demon-possessed man who was blind and mute, and Jesus healed him, so that he could both talk and see. All the people were astonished and said, "Could this be the Son of David?"*
>
> *But when the Pharisees heard this, they said, "It is only by Beelzebul, the prince of demons, that this fellow drives out demons."*
>
> *Jesus knew their thoughts and said to them, "Every kingdom divided against itself will be ruined, and every city or household divided against itself will not stand. If Satan drives out Satan, he is divided against himself. How then can his kingdom stand? And if I drive out demons by Beelzebul, by whom do your people drive them out? So then, they will be your judges. But if it is by the Spirit of God that I drive out demons, then the kingdom of God has come upon you."*

It was pretty handy that Jesus knew their thoughts. He starts asking questions to reveal their illogical thinking. He's basically saying, "How can I be from Satan? I'm casting out Satan." That makes no sense.

He could have just said, *"No, I'm not from Satan."* One sentence. But He didn't do that. He asked questions to get them to think. There were times He answered directly, but not that often.

2. He taught and/or answered questions in parables or analogies.

Rather than answer a question directly, He answered it by telling a story. He did this to get them to think. Here are a few examples from the book of Matthew: 9:14–17; 13:1–52; 20:1–16; 18:1–6 and 21–35; 21:28–22:14; 22:23–33; and 19:16–26.

In Matthew 19:16–26, Jesus was teaching His disciples, and He told them the parable of the rich young ruler.

Just then a man came up to Jesus and asked, "Teacher, what good thing must I do to get eternal life?"

"Why do you ask me about what is good?" Jesus replied. "There is only One who is good. If you want to enter life, keep the commandments."

"Which ones?" he inquired.

Jesus replied, "'You shall not murder, you shall not commit adultery, you shall not steal, you shall not give false testimony, honor your father and mother,' and 'love your neighbor as yourself.'"

"All these I have kept," the young man said. "What do I still lack?"

Jesus answered, "If you want to be perfect, go, sell your possessions and give to the poor, and you will have treasure in heaven. Then come, follow me."

When the young man heard this, he went away sad, because he had great wealth.

Then Jesus said to his disciples, "Truly I tell you, it is hard for someone who is rich to enter the kingdom of heaven. Again, I tell you, it is easier for a camel to go through the eye of a needle than for someone who is rich to enter the kingdom of God."

When the disciples heard this, they were greatly astonished and asked, "Who then can be saved?"

Jesus looked at them and said, "With man this is impossible, but with God all things are possible."

He told this story to expose this man's love of money, to show how he fell short of God's holy standard. The rich young ruler asserted that he obeyed the commandments Jesus mentioned. Jesus answered by saying, *"If you want to be perfect, go, sell your possessions and give to the poor, and you will have treasure in heaven. Then come, follow me."* The young man decided that Jesus was asking too much. Jesus touched on the one issue that proved the man did not measure up to God's holiness. The rich young ruler needed the Savior, and so do we.

The man was not willing to follow the Lord, if that meant he must give up his wealth. He loved himself (and his money) more than the two greatest commandments to love the Lord with all his heart and love his neighbor as himself. Jesus used logical consequences to teach him, and the rich young ruler made his choice.

This is a wonderful example of the way Jesus used parables to stimulate their thinking. And it worked. Those He taught stopped and essentially said, "*Whoa. Wait a minute.*" This caused listeners to think on a deeper level about important issues.

Encourager

JESUS ENCOURAGED HIS followers frequently. He especially encouraged them when they had faith.

Matthew 9:18–22:

> *While he was saying this, a synagogue leader came and knelt before him and said, "My daughter has just died. But come and put your hand on her, and she will live." Jesus got up and went with him, and so did his disciples.*
>
> *Just then a woman who had been subject to bleeding for twelve years came up behind him and touched the edge of his cloak. She said to herself, "If I only touch his cloak, I will be healed."*

Jesus turned and saw her. "Take heart, daughter," he said, "your faith has healed you." And the woman was healed at that moment.

This is such a wonderful model for us. He encouraged their great faith and granted their requests. What an encouragement this is to us to encourage our children when we see character growth in their faith, kindness, honesty, and resilience.

DISCIPLINARIAN

JESUS USED TRUTH and grace as He confronted the woman at the well in John 4:1–29.

Now Jesus learned that the Pharisees had heard that he was gaining and baptizing more disciples than John—although in fact it was not Jesus who baptized, but his disciples. So he left Judea and went back once more to Galilee.

Now he had to go through Samaria. So he came to a town in Samaria called Sychar, near the plot of ground Jacob had given to his son Joseph. Jacob's well was there, and Jesus, tired as he was from the journey, sat down by the well. It was about noon.

When a Samaritan woman came to draw water, Jesus said to her, "Will you give me a drink?" (His disciples had gone into the town to buy food.)

The Samaritan woman said to him, "You are a Jew and I am a Samaritan woman. How can you ask me for a drink?" (For Jews do not associate with Samaritans.)

Jesus answered her, "If you knew the gift of God and who it is that asks you for a drink, you would have asked him and he would have given you living water."

"Sir," the woman said, "you have nothing to draw with and the well is deep. Where can you get this living water? Are you

greater than our father Jacob, who gave us the well and drank from it himself, as did also his sons and his livestock?"

Jesus answered, "Everyone who drinks this water will be thirsty again, but whoever drinks the water I give them will never thirst. Indeed, the water I give them will become in them a spring of water welling up to eternal life."

The woman said to him, "Sir, give me this water so that I won't get thirsty and have to keep coming here to draw water."

He told her, "Go, call your husband and come back."

"I have no husband," she replied.

Jesus said to her, "You are right when you say you have no husband. The fact is, you have had five husbands, and the man you now have is not your husband. What you have just said is quite true."

"Sir," the woman said, "I can see that you are a prophet. Our ancestors worshiped on this mountain, but you Jews claim that the place where we must worship is in Jerusalem."

"Woman," Jesus replied, "believe me, a time is coming when you will worship the Father neither on this mountain nor in Jerusalem. You Samaritans worship what you do not know; we worship what we do know, for salvation is from the Jews. Yet a time is coming and has now come when the true worshipers will worship the Father in the Spirit and in truth, for they are the kind of worshipers the Father seeks. God is spirit, and his worshipers must worship in the Spirit and in truth."

The woman said, "I know that Messiah" (called Christ) "is coming. When he comes, he will explain everything to us."

Then Jesus declared, "I, the one speaking to you—I am he."

Just then his disciples returned and were surprised to find him talking with a woman. But no one asked, "What do you want?" or "Why are you talking with her?"

Then, leaving her water jar, the woman went back to the town and said to the people, "Come, see a man who told me everything I ever did. Could this be the Messiah?"

This is one of my favorite passages of Scripture. Jesus was the perfect combination of grace and truth. He confronted her with compassion as He sensed her open heart to hear what He had to say. He stated the fact of how many husbands she's had without shaming her.

He used strong confrontation as He overturned the tables of the moneychangers as they defiled the temple in John 2:13–22.

> *When it was almost time for the Jewish Passover, Jesus went up to Jerusalem. In the temple courts, he found people selling cattle, sheep and doves, and others sitting at tables exchanging money. So he made a whip out of cords, and drove all from the temple courts, both sheep and cattle; he scattered the coins of the money changers and overturned their tables. To those who sold doves he said, "Get these out of here! Stop turning my Father's house into a market!" His disciples remembered that it is written: "Zeal for your house will consume me."*
>
> *The Jews then responded to him, "What sign can you show us to prove your authority to do all this?"*
>
> *Jesus answered them, "Destroy this temple, and I will raise it again in three days."*
>
> *They replied, "It has taken forty-six years to build this temple, and you are going to raise it in three days?" But the temple he had spoken of was his body. After he was raised from the dead, his disciples recalled what he had said. Then they believed the scripture and the words that Jesus had spoken.*

First, he made a whip and drove out those who were using the temple as a place to sell their goods.

They were defiling it. He overturned their tables and scattered their coins.

He also told them to get out of His Father's temple.

They did not have open hearts.

He used discipline without shame in a variety of ways when He needed to.

NOTICE WHAT'S MISSING

TAKE A LOOK at what types of interactions are missing in the ways Jesus interacted with His people.

1. *Advice Giving:* He doesn't give advice. He lays out the truth and lets people make their own choices. He lets us make mistakes and bad choices. He hopes we will turn to Him for help and learn from our mistakes.

2. *Nagging:* He's not a nagger. He could have nagged the rich young ruler, but He didn't. He could have followed after him as he walked away, saying, *"Are you sure? Come on, go ahead and sell your stuff and you'll have lots of treasure in heaven."* He didn't. He answered his question, and let the rich young ruler decide.

3. *Lecturing:* Jesus didn't lecture. I think of lecturing as trying to discipline through incessant talking. We can go on and on about this and that, and feel like we shared something useful. Think how many times Jesus could have lectured His disciples, *"I've told you a thousand times...why don't you get it?"*

BEING A COMPASSIONATE COACH TO OURSELVES

PART OF COACHING our kids through life includes coaching ourselves to keep ourselves in line, as well as encourage ourselves. It's important to have a dialogue with yourself about what is going on with your children and yourself. It also helps to ask ourselves good questions as we figure out how to parent our children.

I have a little parent-coach on my shoulder most of the time that helps me make good choices about what I do and don't say! Here's what this little part of me that knows better often says,

> *"No. Don't do that. No, don't say that."*
>
> *"Bite your lip. If you say that you'll be sorry."*
>
> *"Think of the long-term consequences. You want a good relationship with them. You want them to visit you when they're older and have children of their own. You don't want to get the mercy phone call at Christmas."*
>
> *"Being a parent is so wonderful and so hard, all at the same time. You're exhausted, and sometimes you have no idea what to do or say. That's okay. Every parent feels this way. Take a few moments to rest, call a friend, or have a good cry."*

One of the benefits of having a compassionate conversation with ourselves is to get us out of reactive mode. It's so easy to yell at our children when they do something horrendous thing. You've told them a million times to not do this, and no sane person would have done this, but they did it anyway! We get mad at them when they have an impulse and take action without taking the time to think it through.

Ideally, a mature person has an impulse, then thinks it through, and then takes action. Often our kids don't do this mature process. Part of this is because their brain isn't mature, some is their sin nature, and part of it is they don't want to stop and think.

Things don't go well when they go straight from impulse to action, and we get mad at them when they do this. However, when we do the same thing and respond impulsively to them without thinking, it may seem okay—like it needed to be said! The reality is that we also need to slow ourselves down when upset, and make sure we think before we respond in ways we later regret. We are most vulnerable to acting impulsively when we are afraid or angry.

Having a compassionate dialog on the inside helps us do just that.

"I have every reason to be upset by what my child did. Any parent would. I'm too upset to talk with her right now. I need to slow myself down and have a conversation in a while when I'm calmer."

FOUR STEPS TO COACH YOUR CHILDREN

Step 1: Ask yourself, *"What do I want my children to remember from this situation?"*

Imagine your son comes home with an "F" on a test. You're tempted out of fear, anger, disappointment, or exhaustion to jump in and tell him what to do, or yell at him for the bad decision he made. As you think about this scenario, ask yourself, *"What do I want my children to remember from this situation?"*

That's a really important question. Most parents are not going to say, *"I want him to remember I screamed at him and told him to go to his room."* That's not a memory any parent would want their child or themselves to have. Your answer will be based on your values and on what's happening in your child's life at the time. Is this his first "F" or his fifteenth "F"? Is he going through something very difficult right now? Does he feel really bad about it, or is he blowing it off?

Let's say your answer to this important question is, "I would want him to know that:

- "I care about him and what he is going through."
- "I know this must be hard for him."
- "I want to help and understand what is going on."
- "It doesn't mean he's a bad person."
- "You're not in this alone."
- "You can come to me even if you made a big mistake."

Step 2: Ask yourself, *"What goals do I have for myself?"*

This means, how you want to conduct yourself, whether you want to discipline with logical consequences versus shame, or how you want to treat yourself with compassion.

Here are some examples:

- "I want to be as calm as possible."
- "I don't want to be reactive."
- "I don't want to say anything I'll be sorry for."
- "I want to do the best imperfect job I can."
- "I want to treat myself with compassion."
- "I want to pray with my children about this problem."

Step 3: Ask yourself, *"What can I do or say right now that will express that?"*

This important question allows you to think of what to say or do to express the important messages you identified in steps one and two.

Based on these goals, here's something I might say,

"Oh an 'F.' I'll bet that was hard to show me. How are you doing? Come over and sit with me. It's not like you to get an 'F,' so something else must be going on. Let's figure this out together."

Later, I would bring up needing to bring the grade up, and a plan to do so. What you come up with is very individual for you as a parent, as well as the unique needs of your child.

Step 4: *Do whatever you decided in steps two and three.*

Now you take action, and do whatever it is you came up with. This looks simple, but often we don't follow through. Instead, we may just react. It helps to have a coach on your shoulder that calms you down and helps you decide what you want to do in the moment based on your values and what you want your children to remember.

Coaching Our Kids by Asking Good Questions

SINCE CHILDREN AND teens tend to not think through all the ramifications of their desires and impulses, a great way to have a positive influence on them is to learn to ask thought-provoking questions. As they ponder these questions, it helps them think through aspects of an issue they may have missed.

It causes their brains to develop as they process both their thoughts and feelings as they wrestle with important issues. During adolescence, our children's brains go through major growth and construction as they reason and make major life decisions. This is a horrifying and scary reality. By asking lots of good questions we also help them take responsibility for the issue at hand. This will help us slowly hand over the reins of their life, so they will be able to make good decisions.

Starting to ask our children thought-provoking questions can begin at a young age. When your four-year-old begs you for a cookie before dinner, you might say, *"Wow, I wonder how hungry you'll be if you eat that cookie?"* Of course, your little one will say, *"I'll be hungry."* Then you respond, *"I know you wish that were true. No cookies before dinner. Would you like one for dessert?"*

Your kids will never say, *"Oh, Mom, I never thought of that. What a great question."*

Not going to happen.

What does happen is that your question stimulates their thinking, even when they're little.

Some Questions to Ask Your Child

WHEN CHILDREN ARE younger, we need to be more direct in our instructions to them. It's also good to add questions here and there as well.

Over time, especially as they get to be tweens and teens, we need to switch to being more of a coach than a teacher.

Asking them good questions helps them develop into independent people. God put a desire in them to become independent so they can leave home and not live with you until they're forty-five! That's a good thing.

As we come alongside them as a coach, we encourage them to think, make decisions, and learn from their mistakes.

There are three basic types of questions that parents can ask to help children's brains mature. Two don't work, and one does!

Investigative Questions

INTENDED TO GET information. It isn't that these are wrong, sometimes we need to get important information. They don't further brain development or independence, so we need to make sure we are asking other questions as well.

- "Where are you going?"
- "Who will be there?"
- "Will your friend's parents be there?"
- "When will you get home?"

Interrogating Questions

INTENDED TO GET information your children or teens may be hiding. Parents sound like cops when they say:

- "Tell me what you're hiding."
- "What really happened?"
- "What did you say? What did he say?"

We ask these types of questions when we are scared. This doesn't work because they will feel threatened and close down inside.

Exploratory Questions

THE BEST KIND of questions are exploratory or coaching questions. These questions are intended to get to know your children and how they are doing on the inside, as well as get them to think. Sometimes we ask questions when we know they should be considering things they haven't thought of.

It's not that they're stupid or unwise, it's that they don't have enough experience to know what to consider.

- "What was it like to give your report today?"
- "How are you doing on the inside?"
- "What was the best part of that for you?"
- "Is there anything else you need to consider before you make your decision?"
- "What's happening with your friendship with Susan?"
- "Is there anything that would get in your way of accomplishing this goal?"
- "What's it like the first day before your first college class?"
- "What's it like having finished your first quarter of college?"
- "What's it like now having sixteen units instead of twelve? Any adjustments you need to make?"
- "I wonder what the fallout will be if you are pulled over by the police and you've been drinking?"
- "What else would you need to be sure of to make your decision?"
- "What consequences might there be?"
- "How might you compensate for the risks?"
- "What would you need to get done first?"
- "How could you make me feel safe about extending your curfew from 10:30 to 11:00?"
- "What resources will you need to accomplish this goal?"
- "What have you tried so far?"
- "What are your options?"
- "How do you think that will work out?"
- "Is there anything that will get in the way of accomplishing this goal?"

- "Where did you find the strength to handle that?"
- "What have you figured out so far?"
- "I wonder what would happen if you say that to your friend?"
- "What else would you need to be sure of to make your decision?"
- "What was enjoyable/challenging/exciting about that?"
- "What caused the most hurt in that situation?"
- "What do you need now? From me? From yourself? From God?"
- "Did that hurt your feelings?"

Here's an example. Your ten-year-old son hasn't been getting his homework done even though you have a homework chart with rewards and remind him. You've done your part, but somehow nothing is working. Rather than lecture him about responsibility and consequences again, you decide to ask some questions to get him involved in coming up with a solution. This time you say, "*What do you think will help you to get your homework done?*"

A question like this might seem absurd, but you'd be surprised. Our kids often come up with ideas we would never think of. Your son ponders and offers ideas, some of which you go for and some you don't, such as:

1. I'll do my homework for twenty minutes on and ten minutes off.
2. I'd like to start with a snack and watch TV for half hour and then start.
3. I need to do it as soon as I get home because I can't go back to it later.
4. I need to relax all afternoon and do it after dinner.

Let's say you nix numbers 2 and 4, but are open to 1 and 3. You might say, *"I'm open to 1 and 3, and you can have a snack with either one of those. Which one do you want to try today?"*

You involved him in brainstorming the question, *"What would work for you? What would make it easier for you to get it done?"* You aren't saying homework is negotiable, or accepting an option you aren't okay with. You are giving him the message that he's responsible for getting his homework done, so think of ways you can be successful.

Here's another example:

Your teenager comes to you with a problem, and says, *"What do you think I should do?"*

You: *"I have some ideas, but what have you figured out so far?"*

My children asked me this question frequently. I wouldn't tell them what I thought in a specific situation, because I had a much greater goal. I wanted to get my children to think for themselves.

I wanted to teach them to trust their thinking, because someday they would grow up and go off on their own. Often when they shared what they came up with, I'd encourage them for what they'd thought of so far.

"Wow, you've really thought about that, that's really great. Sounds like you're going in a good direction."

If they've missed something, I might ask them a good question. Let's say your child comes to you and says, *"I'm really upset about what my friend did today at school. I'm going to send her a text right now and tell her what I think! Grrrrr. I'm going to tell everyone how mad I am on Facebook."*

Parent: [Thinking.] "Hmm. I could give her a lecture and say, *"No you aren't. This is what will happen if you do this.' or tell her, 'You better not put that up there.'"*

Or I could ask some good questions like,

"I wonder what will happen if you say that to your friend?"

"I wonder what would happen if somebody printed out what you said and brought it to school and passed it around. I've heard that can happen."

"That might feel good in the moment. Are there any negatives that could happen to you or your friend if you do?"

"What else could you do about how angry and hurt you are?"

These types of questions help them think through difficult situations and make wise decisions. These are the only types of questions that will invite your children to figure out what's going on inside their heart and share it with you. This will then help your child's brain grow and develop the ability to think through important topics.

If you set up the dots and let your children or teens connect them, they will learn and retain the learning. If we give in to the temptation to lecture or give advice, not only will their brain not grow through the interchange, they will reject what we shared.

We have a lot of wisdom to share that can help our children. We understand many of the situations they face and can anticipate problems. Most of the time the advice we want to give is truly valuable. The issue isn't our wisdom. The issue is that our children need more from us than our answers. They need our wisdom and life experience to ask them the questions that will help them think about options and possible consequences, so they make wise decisions.

TEACH THEM TO THINK LOGICALLY

PART OF COACHING our children to become mature and responsible is to help them think logically. We live in a world where others are continually trying to persuade us to buy their products, vote for their candidate, and believe their political spin. The arguments given are often based on emotions and not on clear thinking.

We can help equip our children to live in the real world by helping them to learn to spot a bad argument or illogical reasoning. It's crucial to help our children step back when given an emotionally laden "fact" and analyze whether it is true or not. It is especially important to help them distinguish between a true statement, a statement the speaker wants us to believe is true, and one that uses fear to convince us is true.

These days, all streams of media are overflowing with statements shared as fact that are untrue. They want us to change our opinion using fear tactics. We need to teach our children ways to think through what is being presented to them and respond properly. There are many people who want to fool us by manipulating our emotions and getting us to agree with something without thinking about it first.

Don't worry if you don't know how to help your children think logically. There are great resources out there for parents and kids to work through together, such as: *The Thinking Toolbox: Thirty-Five Lessons That Will Build Your Reasoning Skills* and *The Fallacy Detective: Thirty-Eight Lessons on How to Recognize Bad Reasoning.*

Now What? Where Do I Start?

1. Seek God for wisdom about how best to coach your children.
2. What did you think of how Jesus taught His followers? How does this inspire you?

3. What type of questions would you like to start asking your children, and how do you think this will help?
4. Does it make sense to help your children think logically? How do you think you could do this in a way that doesn't shame them?
5. Speak to yourself with compassion. *"I'm looking forward to asking my kids good questions. I'm not doing this much at all, and I feel bad about that. It seems so much easier to just tell them what to do. I realize now that doing this isn't helping them learn how to think. It will help me a lot to ask myself what I want my children to remember from interactions with me. I think I'll start asking good questions and see how it goes."*

13

There Are No Guarantees...and Encouragement

Train up a child in the way he should go, even when he is old he will not depart from it.

Proverbs 22:6 (NASB)

I HAVE SEEN many parents hurt when others misapply this verse. It makes me angry. The last thing we need is to blame ourselves for something else. I'd like to explain the meaning of this verse in hopes of providing clarity and assuaging guilt.

Proverbs are sayings that generally true, that generally depict how life goes. Proverbs are not promises. Proverbs are meant to encourage us to live our lives in healthy ways.

I have seen this verse used inaccurately to promise parents that if they raise their children according to the wisdom shared in the Bible, their children will not have problems and will always be true to their faith. I've also seen it used as a way to let parents know that if their children are struggling it must be because they didn't raise them right.

Both of these explanations are false and are very destructive. We love our children, and we do the best we can to raise them the best way we know how. I hope that this book is helpful to you in that regard.

The reality is that there is no guarantee that even if we parent our children with compassion that they will turn out responsible, mature, and remain solid in their faith. We don't have that kind of power.

How we parent is an important part of how they turn out, but there are also many other factors that play into their development, such as:

- Genetics
- Mental illness
- Addictions
- Learning disabilities
- Poverty
- Abuse or neglect
- Physical disabilities
- Prejudice

The good news is that even if your children struggle with some of the above difficulties in life, the compassionate relationship they have with you and with themselves will help them wrestle through the hard times and come out the other side.

What we teach them and how we interact with them softens the hardships they face, teaches them to persevere, and gives them a loving person to walk through life with.

Parenting with compassion gives them a safe place to be themselves, warts and all. A place to learn, fail, and thrive. Whether your family is one of two, five, or ten, we can create a place where they belong, are loved, and feel worthy.

As you've heard throughout this book, we cannot give to our children what we do not have. Your quest to parent with compassion is linked to having compassion for yourself. It is wonderful that we can grow and learn on this journey with our children. Caring for yourself through words and deeds blesses your children as well as yourself.

We can give our children a place to be loved and belong. Focus on being engaged with your children. Pay attention to what's going on in their lives, hearts, and minds. There are lots of ways to parent well.

Be yourself, but be tuned in to your children. If you are too busy, drop what you can. Time and engagement with them is crucial. Get involved with other parents and support one another. We need a community to cheer us on, encourage growth, and relate with compassion.

We're not alone in our parenting struggles.

Let's support and encourage one another and ourselves.

We're in this together—and don't forget the compassion!

ENCOURAGEMENT FOR THE FUTURE

YOU'VE LEARNED SO much as we've walked through this book together. You've worked hard to learn new ways to love yourself and your children.

You've learned the power of compassion in your own life and the lives of your children. You haven't done it perfectly, and you don't need to.

I'm so proud of you for what you've learned, how you've grown, and how you'll continue to grow.

Keep taking care of yourself and talking to yourself with kindness and compassion. You are a precious, imperfect creation of God. Here are a few tips to keep going.

TOP TEN WAYS TO BE YOUR OWN COMPASSIONATE BEST FRIEND

HOW YOU CARE for yourself and speak to yourself is more important than how anyone else treats you. Here are some tips to be that compassionate best friend to yourself you've always wanted.

1. Cling to God. He is there to help you. There may be times you are angry, confused, or feel like turning away from Him. Don't. He is there with open arms. He will give you what you need for the challenges you face as a parent.
2. Talk to yourself kindly…no name calling, blaming, criticism, or put-downs. Regularly ask yourself how you are doing and what you need…and then take steps to practically help yourself.
3. Treat your emotions with respect. When something difficult happens, allow yourself to feel normal emotions and release them in ways that don't hurt you or another person. Allow yourself to grieve. Grieving over the losses and disappointments of life is the secret to getting through life in one piece, with love to spare for yourself and others.
4. Embrace reality. It's hard, I know. When we do, we are able to come up with solutions that can help. There are no solutions when we pretend what's happening isn't happening. As you allow yourself to grieve and care for yourself, you'll be able to handle reality much easier.
5. Say no to ridiculous expectations. No, you can't work, homeschool, lead a women's Bible study, grow your own organic food, be a perfect wife, have a spotless house, and make a meal for someone who is sick.

6. Be compassionate with yourself as you struggle and fail. Forgive yourself for the inevitable mistakes you make as a parent. As we do, it helps our children handle their mistakes more easily.
7. Plan and take time for yourself to rest and recuperate from the stresses of parenting and life you are facing.
8. Practice self-care in areas that fit you. For some this may be healthy eating, exercise that fits you, reading, massage, a long bath, a good run, time with friends, or time alone. Pick what fits you, not someone else.
9. Explore and practice ways to soothe yourself when distressed. You'll be distressed off and on for the rest of your life. Find ways that work to calm yourself.
10. Tell yourself each night what you are proud of yourself for that day…if you look, there are a lot of things you did right!

No doubt you've learned lots of new ways to parent your kids with compassion. Here's a recap to help build a compassionate relationship with your children.

Top Ten Ways to Parent Your Kids with Compassion

WE HAVE AN amazing opportunity to build a close relationship with our children from a foundation of compassion. As we respond to their imperfections with kindness, they will learn to respond to themselves with compassion too. What a gift you are giving them for a lifetime!

1. Be patient, and remember they are young and are learning new things, which means they are constantly failing. It

would be like us showing up to a new job every day and having to learn new things.

2. Rely on God, and turn to Him for help and support. Ask Him to give you compassion for your children and to guide you on how to parent them with grace and truth.
3. Listen and empathize. We bestow the gift of grace to our children when we take the time to listen to them, understand what they are going through, and empathize with their feelings.
4. Discipline with logical consequences, not shame. Our children need us to set clear expectations and boundaries, and to apply logical consequences when they misbehave. This helps them learn right from wrong and gives them practice with how the real world works.
5. Shower them with love and affection. They need concrete ways of soaking in love. Our love can be expressed through physical affection, kind words, listening, and time spent together.
6. Help them understand and express their emotions. When we do, they feel less overwhelmed and out of control. It also helps them accept their feelings and have compassion for what they are going through.
7. Teach your kids how to grieve the losses and disappointments of life. This will help them handle the realities of life and get to a better place emotionally.
8. Show them how to be compassionate with themselves when they fail. This will help them be understanding and accepting of their imperfections. They will learn that life is a process that involves lots of mistakes and that they can grow from them.
9. Coach them with good questions. These questions are intended to get to know your children, how they are doing on the inside, as well as get them to think.

10. Tell your children every day at dinner or bedtime what you are proud of them for. Focus on ways they've grown in character. Examples include: being brave to do something difficult, persevering when they felt like giving up, and showing kindness and compassion to themselves or others.

In Conclusion

Congratulations on reading *Give Your Kids a Break: Parenting with Compassion for You and Your Children*!

I am proud of you and all you've done to form a compassionate relationship with yourself as you parent your children. You've also learned many ways to teach your children to be compassionate with themselves. Keep up the good work! You are valuable, you matter, and you deserve compassion and care…and so do your kids!

Notes

---

[1] Kim Fredrickson, *Give Yourself a Break: Turning Your Inner Critic into a Compassionate Friend* (Grand Rapids, MI: Revell, a division of Baker Publishing Group, 2015), 14. Used by permission.

[2] Neff Kristin, *Self-Compassion* (New York: HarperCollins, 2011), 110.

[3] Kim Fredrickson, *Give Yourself a Break: Turning Your Inner Critic into a Compassionate Friend* (Grand Rapids, MI: Revell, a division of Baker Publishing Group, 2015), 59–61. Used by permission.

[4] J. Stuewig, J.P. Tangney, S. Kendall, J.B. Folk, C.R. Meyer, R.L. Dearing, "Children's Proneness to Shame and Guilt Predict Risky and Illegal Behaviors in Young Adulthood." *Child Psychiatry & Human Development*. 2015, Volume 46, Issue 2, 217–227.

[5] Kristin Neff, *Self-Compassion* (New York: HarperCollins, 2011), 152–154.

[6] John Townsend, "Learning to Bond," in *Unlocking Your Family Patters* by Henry Cloud, John Townsend, Dave Carder, and Earl Henslin (Chicago: Moody Publishers, 2011), 118. Used by permission.

7 Stanley Greenspan, Playground Politics: Understanding the Emotional Life of Your School-Age Child (Boston: Da Capo Press, 1994), 35, 164, 282.

---

[8] Stanley Greenspan, Playground Politics: Understanding the Emotional Life of Your School-Age Child (Boston: Da Capo Press, 1994), 26.

[9] Gary Lundberg, and Joy Lundberg, *I Don't Have to Make Everything All Better* (New York: Penguin Books, 2000), 4, 6.

[10] John Gottman and Joan Declaire, *Raising an Emotionally Intelligent Child: The Heart of Parenting* (New York: Simon and Schuster, 1998), 101.

[11] Daniel Goleman, *Emotional Intelligence: Why it Can Matter More Than IQ* (New York: Bantam Books, 2005).

[12] John Gottman and Joan Declaire, *Raising an Emotionally Intelligent Child: The Heart of Parenting* (New York: Simon and Schuster, 1998), 16–17.

[13] Kim Fredrickson, *Give Yourself a Break: Turning Your Inner Critic into a Compassionate Friend* (Grand Rapids: MI: Revell, a division of Baker Publishing Group, 2015), chapter 7.

[14] Ibid, chapter 9.

[15] John Gottman and Joan Declaire, *Raising an Emotionally Intelligent Child: The Heart of Parenting* (New York: Simon and Schuster, 1998), 101.

[16] Ibid, 27.

[17] John Gottman and Joan Declaire, *Raising an Emotionally Intelligent Child: The Heart of Parenting* (New York: Simon and Schuster, 1998), 21.

[18] Paul Warren and Frank Minirth, *Things That Go Bump in The Night* (Nashville, TN: Thomas Nelson Publishers, 1993), 7. Used by permission.

[19] Ibid, 16.

[20] Karen Dockrey, *When a Hug Won't Fix the Hurt* (Birmingham, AL: New Hope Publishing, 1993), viii. Used by permission.

[21] Ibid, 3–4.

[22] Henry Cloud and John Townsend, *Boundaries with Kids* (Grand Rapids, MI: Zondervan, 2001), 14–15. Used by permission.

Bibliography

Books to Help Parents

Barnill, Julie Ann. *She's Gonna Blow!: Real Help for Mom's Dealing with Anger*. Eugene, OR: Harvest House, 2005.

Berstein, Neil I. *How to Keep Your Teenager Out of Trouble, and What to Do If You Can't*. New York: Workman Publishing Company, 2001.

Brooks, Barbara, and Paul M. Siegel. *The Scared Child*. Hoboken: NJ: John Wiley & Sons, 1996.

Campbell, Ross. *How to Really Love Your Child*. Elgin, IL: David C. Cook, 2015.

Campbell, Ross. *How to Really Love Your Teenager*. Elgin, IL: David C. Cook, 2015.

Campbell, Ross. *Relational Parenting*. Chicago: Moody Press, 2000.

Carder, Dave, Earl Henslin, John Townsend, Henry Cloud, and Alice Brawand. *Unlocking Your Family Patterns*. Chicago: Moody Publishers, 2011.

Carter, Les, and Frank Minirth. *The Anger Workbook*. Thomas Nelson, 2012.

Cline, Foster, and Jim Fay. *Parenting with Love and Logic*. NavPress Publishing, 2006.

Cloud, Henry, and John Townsend. *Boundaries: When to Say Yes, How to Say No to Take Control of Your Life*. Grand Rapids: Zondervan, 1992.

Cloud, Henry, and John Townsend. *Boundaries with Kids*. Grand Rapids, MI: Zondervan, 2001.

Dockery, Karen. *When a Hug Won't Fix the Hurt.* Birmingham: AL: New Hope Publications, 1993.

Eisenberg, Arlene, Heidi Eisenberg Murkoff, and Sandee E. Hathaway. *What to Expect: The Toddler Years*. New York: Workman Publishing Company, 1996.

Faber, Adele, and Elaine Mazlish. *How to Talk So Kids Will Listen and Listen So Kids Will Talk*, New York: Scribner, 2012.

Ford, Judy. *Wonderful Ways to Love a Child.* New York: Fine Communications, 1997.

Fredrickson, Kim. *Give Yourself a Break: Turning Your Inner Critic into a Compassionate Friend.* Grand Rapids, MI: Revell, 2015.

Fredrickson, Kim. *Compassionate Self-Statements and Self-Soothing Exercises* © Kim Fredrickson. CD and mp3 download, 2013. www.cdbaby.com/kimfredrickson

Fredrickson, Kim. *Kind Words to Soothe Your Soul* © Kim Fredrickson. Mp3 download, 2017.
http://www.cdbaby.com/kimfredrickson2

Gentry, Doyle W. *Anger-Free…Ten Steps to Managing Your Anger*. New York: William Morrow Paperbacks, 2000.

Goleman, Daniel. *Social Intelligence: The New Science of Human Relationships*. New York: Bantam, 2007.

Gottman, John. *What Am I Feeling?* Seattle, WA: Parenting Press, 2004.

Gottman, John, and Joan Declaire. *Raising an Emotionally Intelligent Child: The Heart of Parenting*. New York: Simon & Schuster, 1998.

Greenspan, Stanley. *Playground Politics: Understanding the Emotional Life of Your School-Age Child.* Boston: Da Capo Press, 1994.

Lundberg, Gary, and Joy Lundberg. *I Don't Have to Make Everything All Better*. New York: Penguin Books, 2000.

McKay, Matthew, and Patrick Fanning. *When Anger Hurts Your Kids*. Oakland, CA: New Harbinger Publications, 1996.

Moore, Beth. *Praying God's Word*. Nashville, TN: B&H Books, 2009.

Neff, Kristin. *Self-Compassion*. New York: HarperCollins, 2011.

Ramsey, Dave, and Rachel Cruz. *Smart Money Smart Kids: Raising the Next Generation to Win with Money*. Brentwood, TN: Ramsey Press, 2014.

Seamands, David. *Healing for Damaged Emotions*. Elgin, IL: David C. Cook, 2015.

Stoop, David. *Understanding Your Child's Personality*. Carol Stream, IL: Tyndale House Publishers, 2015.

Townsend, John. *Boundaries with Teens*. Grand Rapids, MI: Zondervan, 2006.

VanVonderen, Jeff. *Families Where Grace is the Place*. Minneapolis, MN: Bethany House Publishers, 2010.

Warren, Paul, and Frank Minirth. *Things That Go Bump in The Night*. Nashville, TN: Thomas Nelson, 1993.

Yancey, Philip. *Where is God When It Hurts?* Grand Rapids: Zondervan, 2002.

Books to Help Kids

Agassi, Martine. *Hands Are Not for Hitting*. Golden Valley, MN: Free Spirit Publishing, 2009.

Bang, Molly. *When Sophie Gets Angry—Really, Really Angry*. New York: Scholastic Paperbacks, 2008.

Berry, Joy. *A Children's Book about Throwing Tantrums*. Danbury, CT: Grolier Enterprises, 1988.

Bluedorn, Nathaniel, and Hans Bluedorn. *The Thinking Toolbox: Thirty-Five Lessons That Will Build Your Reasoning Skills*. Christian Logic, 2005.

Bluedorn, Nathaniel, and Hans Bluedorn. *The Fallacy Detective: Thirty-Eight Lessons on How to Recognize Bad Reasoning.* Christian Logic, 2015.

Burkett, Larry. *Money Matters for Teens*. Chicago: Moody Publishers, 2001.

Curtis, Jamie Lee. *Today I Feel Silly*. New York: HarperCollins, 2007.

Cain, Janan. *The Way I Feel*. Seattle, WA: Parenting Press, 2000.

Smith, Bryan. *What Were You Thinking?: Learning to Control Your Impulses*. Boys Town, NE: Boys Town Press, 2016.

Streeter, Merry S. *Lolly's Fish Tale*. Bloomington, IN: AuthorHouse, 2016.

Verdick, Elizabeth, and Marjorie Lisovskis. *How to Take the Grrrr Out of Anger*. Golden Valley, MN: Free Spirit Publishing, 2015.

Wagenbach, Debbie. *The Grouchies.* Washington, DC: Press, 2010.

Also by Kim Fredrickson

Give Yourself a Break:
Turning Your Inner Critic into a Compassionate Friend

Compassionate Self-Statements and Self-Soothing Exercises
to Help You Build a Compassionate Relationship with Yourself
(CD and mp3 download)

Kind and Compassionate Words to Soothe Your Soul
(mp3 download)

Turn the page for more information on these exciting and inspirational works by Kim Fredrickson.

Give Yourself a Break:
Turning Your Inner Critic into
a Compassionate Friend

MANY PEOPLE ARE used to showing compassion to others. What many of us have trouble with is showing that same compassion to ourselves. Too often we say things to ourselves that we would never say to a friend. All this negative self-talk can have a devastating effect on our lives. *Give Yourself a Break* gives you the compassionate words to say to yourself as you negotiate the ups and downs of life.

Applying self-compassion helps us handle our humanness and the situations we are in with empathy, concern, understanding, and kindness. It also gives us the grace to accept and correct our mistakes.

Self-compassion is a gentle way we relate to ourselves, both when we're struggling and when things are going well. We want to treat ourselves as we would a friend who is scared, confused, or learning something new.

Licensed marriage and family therapist Kim Fredrickson wants readers to stop beating themselves up. Grounding her advice in the Bible, she offers practical steps, specific exercises, and compassionate words to say in order to build a loving relationship with ourselves. Through inspiring stories of transformation, she helps us learn to show ourselves the kind of grace and understanding we offer to others—and to change our relationships, our outlook on life, and our view of ourselves in the process.

Compassionate Self-Statements and Self-Soothing Exercises

to Help You Build a Compassionate Relationship with Yourself

CD and mp3 download

https://store.cdbaby.com/cd/kimfredrickson

KIM SHARES KIND and compassionate words to say to yourself as you walk through the ups and downs of life. Learning to talk to yourself as a compassionate friend makes living life a lot easier.

Listen to 34 compassionate self-statements and self-soothing exercises. Kim's soothing voice will help you take in these words of compassion in deeper ways, helping you feel more connected to yourself. It is normal to not know how to speak to yourself with compassion.

This CD offers an opportunity to let truth and grace soak in deeply. You will benefit greatly from reading Kim's book along with listening to this CD.

These tracks provide:

- Examples of how to respond compassionately to yourself when you don't have the words to say.
- Ways to build self-compassion in the areas of self-talk, self-soothing, and self-care.
- Practical exercises and tools you can use to build this relationship with yourself.
- Ways to build inner strength and help heal from life's hurts.
- Words to help fill in the void left by lack of compassion in your life.

We are with ourselves a hundred percent of the time. The way we speak to ourselves has more impact on our well-being than our interactions with others. You matter and are of great worth, no matter what you've done or been through. Listen in to start being a good friend to yourself today! This recording is available as a digital download or on a CD. 80 minutes.

Kind and Compassionate Words to Soothe Your Soul

mp3 download https://store.cdbaby.com/cd/kimfredrickson1

THE MOST IMPORTANT time to be a good friend to yourself is when you are having a hard time. Let these kind and compassionate words warm your soul, soothe your discomfort, increase your joy, and then spread to others naturally.

Allow these words of kindness and compassion soothe your inner critic and help you build a caring relationship with yourself. This recording gives you actual words of kindness and compassion to say to yourself as you live your life.

These Compassionate Messages of Encouragement Include:

- Welcome
- What is self-kindness and self-compassion?
- Talking to yourself with compassion about your mistakes
- Changing your negative self-talk

- Kind words about the mistakes you make as a parent
- Compassion about struggling with life and relationships
- Feeling discouraged by your limitations
- Compassion for not taking care of yourself
- Compassion as you go through transitions and adjustments
- Struggling to believe you are of value
- Treating yourself with warmth, empathy, and respect
- Helping young kids talk to themselves kindly when they mess up
- Self-compassion for teens
- Comforting scriptures during tough times
- Closing and encouragement